The Performance of

Foreign-Owned Firms in Canada

by
A. E. Safarian

CANADIAN-AMERICAN COMMITTEE
sponsored by
National Planning Association (U.S.A.)
Private Planning Association of Canada

Legal Deposit — 3rd Quarter 1969
Quebec National Library

Library of Congress Catalog Card Number: 72-88570

1969, $2.00

National Planning Association (Washington, D.C.) and
Private Planning Association of Canada (Montreal, Que.)

Printed in Canada

THE CANADIAN-AMERICAN COMMITTEE

The Canadian-American Committee was established in 1957 to study problems arising from growing interdependence between Canada and the United States. With approximately equal representation from coast to coast in the two countries, its members are business, labour, agriculture, and professional leaders. The Committee is sponsored by two non-profit research organizations — the National Planning Association in the United States and the Private Planning Association of Canada.

The Committee believes that good relations between Canada and the United States are essential for the future prosperity, and perhaps even the survival, of both countries. It is therefore seeking not only to encourage a better understanding of the problems which have arisen and may arise, but also to develop solutions for such problems which are in the common interest of both countries. The Committee is taking a North American approach in its search for constructive programs.

The Committee is sponsoring a series of objective research studies on various aspects of Canadian-American relations. These are being undertaken by qualified experts in both countries and, with the Committee's approval, will be published. On the basis of these factual studies and of discussions at its meetings, the Committee also issues policy statements signed by its members. Such statements are directed at increasing public understanding of the attitudes, policies, and actions which the Committee believes would best serve the mutual interests of the peoples of both countries.

The Canadian-American Committee is a unique organization, both in terms of its broadly diversified membership and in terms of its blending of factual studies and policy conclusions on Canadian-American relations. It meets twice a year, once in Canada and once in the United States. Its work is jointly financed by funds contributed from private sources in the United States and Canada and by foundation grants.

Offices on behalf of the Committee are maintained at 1606 New Hampshire Avenue, N.W., Washington, D.C. 20009, and at 757 Sun Life Building, Montreal, Quebec. John Miller (Assistant Chairman and Executive Secretary of NPA) serves as Secretary of the Committee. T.L. Powrie, in Montreal, and Sperry Lea, in Washington, are the Directors of Research.

Robert M. Fowler Harold W. Sweatt

Co-chairmen of the Committee

iii

STATEMENT
BY THE CANADIAN-AMERICAN COMMITTEE
ON *The Performance of Foreign-Owned Firms in Canada*

With this publication, the Canadian-American Committee returns to examining the operations of foreign-owned — principally U.S.-owned — subsidiaries in Canada. An early study sponsored by the Committee, *Policies and Practices of U.S. Subsidiaries in Canada* by John Lindeman and Donald Armstrong, pioneered scrutiny of various aspects of the performance of these subsidiaries.

For some time now, the Committee has sought to foster further steps in the study of this question. Our purposes, similar to those animating the previous publication, are to stimulate different and better subsidiary performance where this is warranted and to provide a more factual basis for discussion of an important subject. We were fortunate that Professor A. E. Safarian of the University of Toronto agreed to a publication by the Committee of an updated and revised paper he had prepared on this topic.

The present report advances the investigation and discussion in several respects. It considers not only corporate behaviour as such, but also the economic effects of this behaviour on Canada. The author has brought to bear considerable new data developed by himself and by others. The scope of the present study is broadened beyond U.S. subsidiaries to include all foreign-owned companies in Canada as well as resident-owned firms. And, for the sake of comparison, it summarizes the findings of comparable research on the performance of U.S.-owned subsidiaries in the United Kingdom and Australia.

In focusing on "performance," Professor Safarian develops conclusions on those consequences of foreign ownership that have often been the subject of criticism in Canada and elsewhere. Subsidiary performance is often thought to be adversely affected by such phenomena as conflicts of interest between the subsidiaries and their foreign parents, to the detriment of their contributions to the Canadian economy and society. (The particular claims covered in this study are outlined on pages 3-4.)

As we see them, Professor Safarian's basic findings fall into the two groups indicated by his own summary statement that "Canadians may have been worrying too much about some things and not enough about others."

1. If we limit our considerations to the results of managerial decisions based solely on business criteria, the actual performance of foreign-owned subsidiaries in Canada is seen to be little different from that of comparable Canadian-owned firms. Although there do exist cases of inferior performance, they usually represent either a small minority of foreign-owned firms or a larger proportion

of foreign-owned and Canadian-owned firms alike. Thus, within the sphere of purely business-motivated behaviour, the economic performance of firms within Canada is primarily determined, not by nationality of ownership, but by the economic and social environment, and particularly by the Canadian policy environment, within which all firms alike — however owned — must operate in Canada. The key to both improved performance of all Canadian firms and fuller economic benefits from foreign investment is to be found in a more appropriate set of Canadian trade and other industrial policies — aimed at achieving more specialization and entrepreneurship in Canadian manufacturing industries for a larger and more competitive market.

2. But the fact of foreign ownership — or of U.S. ownership — has, at times, disturbed or threatened the performance of subsidiaries in Canada — along with evoking political feelings and questions there. In these cases the process has originated, not in U.S. corporate business decisions, but in U.S. laws and policies that are extended to Canada through the medium of the subsidiaries. Three examples are the U.S. restriction on exports by American-controlled foreign affiliates to certain Communist countries, the application of U.S. anti-trust laws within Canada, and (for a time) capital restraint programs to moderate private capital transactions in the U.S. balance of payments.

We agree, then, with Professor Safarian's analysis that Canadians have worried too much about those influences on subsidiary performance that originate in the ordinary business decisions of foreign management but have worried too little about, first, the significance of Canadian trade and other industrial policies and, second, the transmittal to Canada of U.S. governmental regulations via the link of foreign ownership.[1]

The Committee states its support for the view developed in this study, namely, that extraterritoriality is the area in which the most serious Canadian-American conflicts of interest have arisen and are most likely to arise and in which solutions most need to be found.

In view of the enormous growth of U.S. direct investment in other countries, we also urge that the United States government review comprehensively its practices relating to the extraterritorial application of its laws and regulations to the foreign activities of U.S. companies.

---

[1] See footnotes by David Kirk and Claude Ryan on following page.

May, 1969

Footnotes to the Statement

David Kirk: It is important to re-emphasize, which the Committee Statement does not, Dr. Safarian's own concluding emphasis (page 107) that in his study "no attempt has been made to analyze systematically such matters as balance of payments effects, political effects, or over-all benefits and costs, all of which deserve fuller examination."

Claude Ryan: I agree, then, that in the present state of our knowledge on this complex matter, this conclusion is justifiable. I consider, however, that there is still some important evidence to be gathered on this subject and that pending further progress we must avoid indulging in false complacency.

MEMBERS OF THE CANADIAN-AMERICAN COMMITTEE
SIGNING THE STATEMENT

Co-chairmen

ROBERT M. FOWLER
President, Canadian Pulp and
Paper Association

HAROLD W. SWEATT
Honorary Chairman of the
Board, Honeywell Inc.

Members

T. N. BEAUPRE
Chairman of the Board and
President, Domtar Limited

T. J. BELL
President, Abitibi Paper
Company Ltd.

E. D. BROCKETT, JR.
Chairman of the Board,
Gulf Oil Corporation

EARL L. BUTZ
Vice President for Special Projects,
Purdue Research Foundation

FRANCOIS E. CLEYN
President, Cleyn & Tinker Ltd.

THOMAS E. COVEL
Vice President, Aluminium
Limited, Inc.

WILLIAM DODGE
Secretary-Treasurer,
Canadian Labour Congress

A. D. DUNTON
President, Carleton University

H. E. EKBLOM
Senior Vice President,
The Chase Manhattan Bank

MARCEL FARIBAULT
Montreal, Quebec

J. R. FLUOR
President, Fluor Corporation, Ltd.

HAROLD S. FOLEY
Vancouver, British Columbia

JOHN F. GALLAGHER
Vice President, International
Operations, Sears, Roebuck and Co.

G. H. GALLAWAY
President, Crown Zellerbach
International, Inc.

CHAS. W. GIBBINGS
President, Saskatchewan Wheat Pool

ARTHUR R. GIBBONS
Executive Secretary, Canadian
Railway Labour Executives'
Association

WILFRED N. HALL
Como, Quebec

F. PEAVEY HEFFELFINGER
Honorary Chairman of the Board &
Member of the Executive Committee,
Peavey Company

vii

GILBERT W. HUMPHREY
Chairman,
The Hanna Mining Company

CURTIS HUTCHINS
Chairman of the Board,
Dead River Company

R. A. IRWIN
President, Consolidated-Bathurst Ltd.

CRAWFORD T. JOHNSON
Assistant to the Chairman,
Baker Industries

VERNON E. JOHNSON
Calumet, Quebec

JOSEPH D. KEENAN
International Secretary, International
Brotherhood of Electrical Workers,
AFL-CIO

*DAVID KIRK
Executive Secretary, The Canadian
Federation of Agriculture

W. S. KIRKPATRICK
Chairman & Chief Executive Officer,
Cominco Ltd.

WILLIAM LADYMAN
International Vice-President,
International Brotherhood of Electrical
Workers, AFL-CIO-CLC

HERBERT H. LANK
Director, Du Pont of Canada, Limited

FRANKLIN A. LINDSAY
President, Itek Corporation

DONALD MacDONALD
President, Canadian Labour Congress

ROBERT P. MacFADDEN
Vice President, First National
City Bank

ROBERT M. MacINTOSH
Deputy Chief General Manager,
The Bank of Nova Scotia

M. W. MACKENZIE
Como, Quebec

W. A. MACKINTOSH
Kingston, Ontario

WILLIAM MAHONEY
National Director, United Steelworkers
of America, AFL-CIO-CLC

BROOKS McCORMICK
Executive Vice President,
International Harvester Company

JOSEPH MORRIS
Executive Vice President,
Canadian Labour Congress

KENNETH D. NADEN
Executive Vice President,
National Council of Farmer
Cooperatives

THOMAS S. NICHOLS
Chairman of the Executive Committee,
Olin Mathieson Chemical Corporation

JOSEPH E. NOLAN
Senior Vice President—Administration,
Weyerhaeuser Company

I. H. PECK
President, Canadian International
Paper Company

MARCEL PEPIN
National President, Confederation
of National Trade Unions

CHARLES PERRAULT
Conseil du Patronat du Québec

JAY RODNEY REESE
President, Texas Instruments
Supply Company

CHARLES RITZ
Honorary Chairman of the Board,
International Milling Company, Inc.

HOWARD I. ROSS
Touche, Ross, Bailey & Smart

HENRY E. RUSSELL
President, Carling Brewing Company

THOMAS W. RUSSELL, JR.
First Vice President, Abex
Corporation

*CLAUDE RYAN
Publisher-Editor, *Le Devoir*

KARL E. SCOTT
President, Ford Motor Company of
Canada, Limited

LEROY D. SMITHERS
President, Dow Chemical of Canada,
Limited

H. CHRISTIAN SONNE
New York, New York

CLAUDE O. STEPHENS
Chairman of the Board, Texas
Gulf Sulphur Company, Incorporated

JAMES A. SUFFRIDGE
International President Emeritus,
Retail Clerks International
Association, AFL-CIO

WILLIAM I. M. TURNER, JR.
President, Power Corporation
of Canada, Limited

W. O. TWAITS
President, Imperial Oil Limited

JOHN R. WHITE
Vice President and Director,
Standard Oil Company (New Jersey)

HENRY S. WINGATE
Chairman, The International Nickel
Company of Canada, Limited

FRANCIS G. WINSPEAR
Edmonton, Alberta

DAVID J. WINTON
The Winton Company

ARNOLD S. ZANDER
Green Bay, Wisconsin

*See Footnotes to the Statement, page vi.

AUTHOR'S FOREWORD

A portion of the material contained in this study appeared in more extended form in my book, *Foreign Ownership of Canadian Industry*, published by McGraw-Hill Company of Canada Limited in 1966. The present study incorporates new data which have become available since my book was completed, and also includes some comparisons with the performance of American-owned companies in several other countries.

An earlier version of this study was prepared for the Task Force on the Structure of Canadian Industry.

I am grateful to the staff of the Canadian-American Committee for their assistance in preparing the manuscript for publication. The entire responsibility for what appears in the study rests with the author.

A. E. Safarian
April, 1969

CONTENTS

TABLES

CHARTS

FRONTISPIECE

NATIONALITY OF CONTROL OF CAPITAL INVESTED IN SELECTED CANADIAN INDUSTRIES, YEAR ENDS, 1926, 1957, AND 1963

		Foreign control		Canadian control
		United States	other	
Manufacturing	1926	30%	5%	65%
	1957	43%	13%	44%
	1963	46%	14%	40%
Petroleum and natural gas	1926	Separate data not available		
	1957	70%	6%	24%
	1963	62%	12%	26%
Other mining and smelting	1926	32%	6%	62%
	1957	52%	9%	39%
	1963	52%	7%	41%
Railways	1926	3%		97%
	1957	2%		98%
	1963	2%		98%
Other utilities	1926	20%		80%
	1957	4%	1%	95%
	1963	4%		96%
Total of above industries and merchandising	1926	15%	2%	83%
	1957	27%	5%	68%
	1963	27%	7%	66%

Data from Dominion Bureau of Statistics, *The Canadian Balance of International Payments 1963, 1964 and 1965 and International Investment Position* (Ottawa: Queen's Printer, 1967), p. 127. A number of changes in coverage, concepts and construction have occurred over the years. The foreign control ratios measure equity and debt capital invested by residents as well as non-residents in those companies whose voting stock is controlled by non-residents, all of which is taken as a percentage of the total capital employed in the industries.

1

Introduction
and Summary of Conclusions

Introduction

It has long been recognized that direct investment conveys both benefits and costs to the receiving country. The benefits consist, in the first instance, in the receipt of capital, of techniques of various kinds, and of market contacts. The costs involve the payment of interest, dividends, and fees for business services; they also involve the need, faced by any nation living in an open economy, to so order its affairs as to maintain equilibrium in its international payments over time.

The "Performance" Question

Over the past decade, Canadians have increasingly questioned another aspect of foreign direct investment, namely, the "performance" of subsidiary firms located in Canada.

In this connection, what do Canadians mean by performance? The intended meaning goes far beyond the usual concept of profitability and includes a number of other aspects of the subsidiaries' operations which significantly affect Canadians. Among these aspects are, for example, the levels and growth of production, the sources of financing and of inputs of goods and services, the destination of finished products, the nationality composition of senior personnel, and the distribution between the subsidiary and its foreign parent of the powers to make decisions and of the facilities to do research. Canadian concern over performance extends beyond the question of what all these operations may imply for the subsidiaries themselves; it focuses, indeed, on the question of what

1

contributions the firms so operating may make, or fail to make, to Canadian society and the Canadian economy. In certain aspects, the performance of subsidiaries can be measured objectively against that of other firms in Canada or abroad, but in some aspects, as we shall see, the performance can be judged only in terms of more subjective criteria.

It is often suggested that the performance of foreign-owned subsidiaries in Canada, and thus of the Canadian economy in which they operate, is adversely affected by conflicts of interest and of outlook — whether actual or potential — between the subsidiary and its parent company. Two reasons are usually offered for these conflicts:

1. In the first place, it is often claimed, decisions that may appear reasonable and profitable from the standpoint of the foreign-based international firm may conflict with the interests of the Canadian subsidiary. The argument runs that, to the extent that the international firm may try to maximize its global profit over time, it may not necessarily foster or permit the maximum feasible development of the subsidiary company.

2. It is sometimes also claimed that the centralization of some key decisions in the international firm may work against the interests of the subsidiary and of the Canadian economy if for no other reason than that head office personnel may be insufficiently informed about, or insufficiently interested in achieving, the subsidiary's potential, while retaining some power over decisions affecting it. It has even been suggested that head office personnel give preference to the development of the parent company — sometimes in consistency with maximizing the profit of the over-all firm, but sometimes not — and that, in any event, changes favouring the subsidiary are difficult to bring about in a complex international organization in which the interests of many affiliated firms must be considered.

Such beliefs have found expression in many government and private statements by Canadians which assert that foreign-owned firms must act as good corporate citizens. These beliefs appear also to be part of the basis for recent Canadian legislation regarding such firms, such as the tax benefits which the budget of June, 1963, offered to companies with specified minimum proportions of Canadian ownership and resident directors. Since 1965, moreover, the view that the performance of Canadian subsidiaries leaves something to be desired has been greatly strengthened by the U.S. government's practice of issuing "guidelines" to parent companies urging them to operate their subsidiaries in ways which, from the Canadian viewpoint, would impair their performance. The Canadian government, in turn, has issued its own guiding principles to the subsidiaries, and it has begun to scrutinize the statistical results of their operations more closely than in the past.

If the indicated Canadian beliefs are well-founded, then there are significant further disadvantages to Canada from foreign direct investment — disadvantages which would have to be weighed against the economic benefits and costs noted in the opening paragraph.

Unfortunately, the controversy over performance has been carried on, for the most part, with limited information or none at all. Controversy on so important a subject, without adequate facts, is bound to produce great heat and little light. This study is an attempt to provide a factual basis for the discussion by bringing together the available information on the operations of foreign-owned firms in Canada.

Scope of the Study

We have selected for analysis some of the more important Canadian criticisms about the performance of foreign-owned firms. The aspects of performance examined here do not include all those that have raised concern; limitations of data, in particular, have prevented a more exhaustive analysis.

It is claimed that many foreign-owned firms with direct investment in Canada

a) limit the opportunities for Canadians to serve in senior management ranks and on the boards of their Canadian subsidiaries.
b) limit severely the decision-making permitted to the Canadian subsidiaries.
c) prevent the subsidiary from being export-oriented, except in the case of raw materials, to avoid its competing with the parent and perhaps other affiliates abroad.
d) require the subsidiary to buy from its parent or other foreign affiliates, or from such affiliates' foreign suppliers, to the detriment of Canadian production of these items.
e) centralize their research and development facilities in the parent company, thus inhibiting research spending, along with the employment of scientific personnel, in Canada.
f) adopt financial policies that give precedence to the needs of the parent, thus involving the subsidiary in heavy payments abroad as well as in the pricing of exports and imports contrary to Canadian interests.
g) are not as efficient as they might be and consequently supply products and services in Canada at higher costs than necessary.

Common to these views is the idea that decisions about Canadian-based facilities, made in the context of the international firm, may lead to something less than the maximum efficient development possible and may also tend to bias the development of the Canadian economy against secondary manufactures and certain kinds of expenditure, such as those on research.

In all but one section, the kind of decision-making whose result concerns us is private decision-making within the international firm. We recognize, of course, that such decisions are made in the context of given sets of laws in Canada and abroad. It is obvious that governments can also affect performance directly. The issues raised by such governmental decision-making, particularly those relating to the extraterritorial extension of foreign laws and regulations through the subsidiaries, will be considered in the final section.

The Approach of the Study

Let us admit at the outset that an empirical study of the performance question, in the ultimate sense, is not possible. We do not know, nor can we reconstruct, what the present performance of the Canadian economy would be if there had been no foreign investment. The answers to any theoretical work involving the rewriting of one hundred years or more of economic history would depend heavily on speculation as to the domestic policies that would have been followed in the absence of foreign investment.

The actual facts regarding the operations of foreign-owned firms as they now exist in Canada can be given, of course. Such data in isolation, however, tell us nothing about desirable performance or even feasible performance. In addition, it is absolutely essential to have a group or groups of firms with which comparisons can be made if we are to find these data meaningful and, specifically, if we are to judge the extent to which the performance of foreign-owned firms accords with, or can accord with, the development objectives of Canadian governments. Therefore, this study will make comparisons, where possible, with resident-owned Canadian firms, with parent companies, and with the performance of U.S. direct investment companies in some other countries for which data are available (notably Australia and the United Kingdom). Distinctions will also be made between firms that are wholly foreign-owned and those that have a degree of Canadian ownership.

It need hardly be emphasized that decision-making within the international firm is a very complex process. We do not attempt here to summarize the literature on this subject. Our concern, rather, is to attempt to quantify the end results of the decision-making process, analyzing the process only so far as this seems necessary for the task set out above.

The Nature of the Available Data

It should be made clear that the data available on the performance of foreign-owned firms, and indeed on that of Canadian firms as well, are extremely limited. Much of it was collected for other purposes and can only with difficulty be adapted to the present purpose. A brief comment in an appendix on the nature of available data in this field will serve to warn the reader of the limitations of the present study.

No comprehensive original statistics have been prepared for the present study. It relies very largely on examination of the information discussed in the appendix, on analysis of some related information, and on a few special tabulations. Within the time available for the present study, it proved quite impossible to prepare comprehensive original estimates to answer many questions on which there is still doubt regarding the operations of the companies concerned.

The plan for each of the seven substantive sections of this report is to outline the major questions that have been raised in Canada about the performance of foreign-owned firms and to present the available data. Their performance thus measured will then be compared (data permitting) with that of resident-owned firms, that of parent companies, that of U.S. direct investment firms elsewhere, and as between Canadian subsidiaries that are wholly owned by the parent and those that are not. An attempt will be made to relate these comparisons to Canadian national interests.

Summary of Conclusions

Available data and analysis are still far from adequate. But they do suggest that Canadians have been worrying too much about certain things and not enough about others.

The performance of foreign-owned subsidiaries in Canada is so varied that general criticisms of them usually do not stand up to statistical examination. Where behaviour that has been defined as undesirable by public authorities does appear, it can often be related more closely to aspects of the economic environment of the subsidiary and only distantly, if at all, to the fact of foreign ownership.

Foreign-owned firms obviously differ, because of their links with the parent, from firms owned by Canadian residents. Such links create special costs that need to be minimized, and also special benefits that need to be maximized, if Canada is to derive as much net gain as possible from foreign direct investment. Problems arise that are peculiar to direct investment, such as the informal arrangements within some international firms to restrict the markets of their affiliates and the need to minimize income paid abroad. There are also special opportunities to be maximized that arise from the links with the parent. These opportunities pertain to much more than the availability of capital and include also such actual or potential advantages as the access to a wide range of techniques and to market contacts.

Actual economic performance of subsidiary companies in Canada often does not differ greatly, however, from that of resident-owned companies. Performance is very similar between the two groups in regard to, for example, exports and research, and it is not markedly less favourable in regard to imports. When we turn to comparisons with the parent, however, we find that subsidiaries are usually less efficient. In the manufacturing sector, many subsidiaries are relatively small firms producing virtually the full range of products identical to those of the parent. Their unit costs of production exceed those of the parent in most cases. This inefficient structure of industry reflects, fundamentally, the limitations on market and firm size, and on specialization, resulting from Canadian and foreign tariffs and from lack of competition in Canada.

Similar or worse problems afflict many firms in the resident-owned sector of manufacturing. Improvement would be desirable in the performance of Canadian firms generally, whatever the sources of their ownership. It would require rationalization of industrial structure in the direction of greater scale and specialization, including that for export. While Canadians have received a great deal of foreign direct investment, they have been receiving too little of its potential benefits, because of inappropriate industrial policies.

As noted above, a high degree of foreign ownership implies some special problems and some special opportunities. The findings of this study suggest that a high degree of foreign ownership is not necessarily, by itself, a general barrier to improvement in performance. This is suggested by the similarities in the performance of foreign-owned and resident-owned firms in roughly comparable circumstances, as well as by the variation in performance that evidently accompanies variation in other basic determinants besides ownership and by the superior performance that direct investment firms in some other countries show when compared with those in Canada.

While Canadians have worried too much about the effects of private decision-making within international firms, they have not given sufficient thought to the serious questions raised by the extraterritorial extension of U.S. laws and government regulations to Canada through the medium of subsidiary firms. Subsidiary performance is affected and, more important, Canadian independence is impaired, by restrictions on exports by subsidiaries to certain countries, by the mandatory balance of payments guidelines applied to Canada for several months early in 1968, and by the extension of U.S. anti-trust decisions to subsidiaries in Canada. If satisfactory multilateral or bilateral solutions are not found to these and similar problems, the stakes may eventually be considered sufficiently important that governments will resort to unilateral and probably second-best solutions.

2

Characteristics of the Managers and the Boards of the Foreign-Owned Firms

Do foreign-owned firms in Canada discriminate against the employment of Canadians? More particularly, do they discriminate in this way in their senior positions? No absolute test of this question can be made on the basis of present information; to our knowledge, the question itself has never been phrased in quite this form in any of the available studies. What the available data do permit us to say is that Canadians are widely represented in the senior positions of most foreign-owned firms in Canada, yet are not so represented in a significant minority of them.

Situation in Canada

An official U.S. study concluded that, in 1957, only 3 percent of the supervisory, professional, and technical personnel in U.S. direct investment companies in Canada (1,000 individuals out of 35,000) had been sent from the United States, but an even smaller proportion — well under one percent — of the other employees in these firms.[1]

With reference to senior management, Canadian data are available for 1962 for all the 138 manufacturing, mining, and petroleum corporations whose assets were $25 million or more and whose stock was owned 50 percent or more

---

[1] U.S. Department of Commerce, *U.S. Business Investments in Foreign Countries* (1960), p. 122.

abroad.[2] In 75 percent of these companies (103 firms) the president was resident in Canada, and in 45 percent of them (62 firms) he was a Canadian citizen. Fully 82 percent of the other officers resident in Canada (706 out of 865) were Canadian citizens. By contrast, in these same industries, in the 79 corporations whose stock was mainly held in Canada and whose assets were over $25 million, only 9 percent of the presidents who were resident in Canada were not Canadian citizens, and only 5 percent of the other officers resident in Canada did not have Canadian citizenship (see Table 1).

Safarian's study of 280 foreign-owned companies in Canada,[3] both large and small, found that many did not have a board chairman or a president as such. Table 2 indicates the main results of that study. It shows that the chairman of the board of a Canadian company, where such a position exists, is most often a national of the parent's country. About half the presidents are nationals of Canada, and almost two-thirds of the next three senior officers. However, there were 57 firms (21 percent) — including a number that were of large and medium size — in which the next three senior officers were all nationals of the country of the parent company. The percentage of presidents who were nationals of Canada increased markedly as the size of the firm increased and somewhat less markedly as the age of the firm increased. It should be added that the data on nationality of senior personnel conceal groups of persons with very different lengths of residence in Canada, varying all the way from what have become lifetime appointments to a relatively short tour of duty in Canada.

TABLE 1

OFFICERS IN CANADA OF 217 MANUFACTURING AND MINING
CORPORATIONS WITH ASSETS OVER $25 MILLION IN 1962
(number of persons)

Degree of Non-Resident Ownership	Number of Corporations	President		Other Officers	
		Resident in Canada	Resident and a Canadian Citizen	Resident in Canada	Resident and a Canadian Citizen
95% and over	94	66	39	519	418
75-94.9%	21	19	10	177	144
50-74.9%	23	18	13	169	144
25-49.9%	22	21	20	162	159
5-24.9%	39	38	35	345	334
Under 5%	18	18	17	119	101
Total	217	180	134	1,491	1,300

Source: CALURA, *Report for 1962,* p.36.

---

[2] Corporations and Labour Unions Returns Act (hereafter referred to as CALURA), *Report for 1962* (1965), p. 36.
[3] A. E. Safarian, *Foreign Ownership of Canadian Industry* (Toronto: McGraw-Hill Company of Canada Ltd., 1966), pp. 50-71.

CHART 1

CANADIAN OFFICERS IN 217 MANUFACTURING AND MINING CORPORATIONS WITH ASSETS OVER $25 MILLION IN 1962

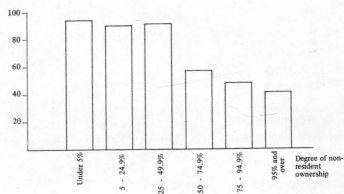

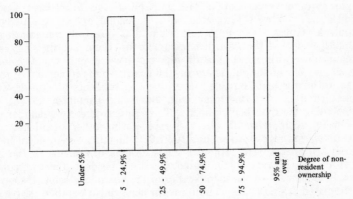

Source: Derived from Table 1.

TABLE 2

CHARACTERISTICS OF SENIOR OFFICERS
OF 280 SUBSIDIARIES
(number of persons)

	Chairman of Board	President	Next Three Officers	Total Persons
Resident in Canada	50	158	591	798
Non-resident	76	85	174	333
No such officer	34	10	–	44
Inactive board	63	–	–	63
No response to question	57	27	(12)[a]	–
Total	280	280		
Number of *residents* formerly employed with parent or its affiliates abroad	11	60	122	193
Number of persons (wherever resident) who are nationals of country of parent	74	119	286	476

[a] Number of companies.

Source: A.E. Safarian, *Foreign Ownership of Canadian Industry,* pp. 53-60.

As for the boards of the subsidiary companies, it must be noted that very often these are set up simply to meet legal requirements and do not exercise any active role in the affairs of the subsidiary. Safarian's study concluded that the boards of almost one-quarter of the firms studied were not active, and that a significant portion of the remainder were not particularly active. For those that were described as active, the total number of directors was 1,505. Four broad groups of directors can be distinguished in this total. First, there were 634 directors who were associated with the parent or with the parent's affiliates outside Canada. Second, there were 565 directors representing the senior management of the Canadian company on these boards. Only seven of the companies with active boards did not have a representative of the senior management of the subsidiary on the board. Third, 40 percent of the firms with active boards had "outside" directors, i.e., residents of Canada who were not associated in any other way with either the parent or any of its affiliates, including the Canadian company. These outside directors numbered 221 in all. Finally, there were 85 directors representing other significant owners, legal counsel, and so on. About half the 1,505 directors were resident in Canada, and only ten boards were without a single resident of Canada. Of the 208 concerns with active boards, 33 indicated that their resident directors constituted less than 25 percent of the membership of the board — which Canadian law in 1963 stipulated as one of the conditions for achieving a required degree of Canadian ownership for certain tax purposes.

Relation to Ownership

One of the questions that has often arisen is whether there is any association between, on the one hand, the extent to which the parent holds the voting stock of the Canadian subsidiary and, on the other hand, other aspects of performance. Such an association does exist in connection with certain of the nationality and residence characteristics: the extent to which presidents are Canadian nationals and the extent to which directors reside in Canada both rise as the degree of parental ownership of the voting stock falls.[4]

In comparing resident-owned and non-resident-owned companies, an important difference exists in the composition of senior personnel and of boards. In regard to firms with assets of $1 million or more, it was found that fully 40 percent of the directors of the non-resident-owned firms were associated with the foreign affiliates, a group that would be absent for the resident-owned firms. The difference between the two sets of firms is highlighted by the presence of substantially more "outside" directors[5] in the resident-owned firms. To express these findings in another way, the boards of non-resident-owned companies are much more strongly representative of management interests, whether managers of the parent or managers of the subsidiary.[6]

Comparison with Australia and the United Kingdom

In the 96 American-owned Australian companies studied by Brash[7] for the year 1962, 38 percent of the board members (224 of 590) were Americans. Of these, only fifty lived in Australia. Even among the wholly American-owned companies, the Australian directors were generally in a majority. The afore-mentioned 50 resident American directors and 146 other Americans constituted the entire group of resident Americans associated with the 96 subsidiary companies and eight unincorporated branches. These firms had a total work force of 75,597 in 1962. Of the 146 Americans who were not resident directors, fewer than half were in executive positions. The 196 persons making up the whole resident American group were concentrated in a few firms: 63 companies employed no Americans and had no resident American directors; 17 companies employed one American or had one resident American director; and fully 124 Americans were shared among seven companies.

---

[4] The differences that are apparent for varying degrees of parental ownership are statistically significant and not due to chance. The test used here and elsewhere is referred to as the chi-square test. Essentially what is involved in this test is that the actual observed frequency with which the data fall into particular groups is compared with an expected frequency based on a distribution due to chance. The test centres on the closeness between the observed and expected frequencies. One does not prove definitively that the difference between the two distributions was due to chance factors alone, but one can make a judgment based on the probability that the difference would have occurred. A 5 percent level of significance was used in the present study.

[5] "Outside" directors are, as defined earlier, residents of Canada not associated in any other way with the over-all company.

[6] Safarian, *op. cit.*, pp. 54-56, 258, 270.

[7] Donald T. Brash, *American Investment in Australian Industry* (Canberra: Australian National University Press, 1966).

These proportions of American executives and directors in Australia are substantially lower than in Canada, even taking account of the fact that the data on Australia include a significant minority of firms in which the American ownership is 25-49 percent. Moreover, the distance from the United States means that there are far fewer personal visits by executives of the American parent firms than in the case of Canada. Possibly in order to compensate for this lack of direct contact, there appears to be more-detailed and more-frequent reporting to the parent than in the case of Canada.[8]

As for the United Kingdom, Dunning notes that about one in four American firms are headed by an American managing director. Moreover, American nationals formed a majority of the board of directors in less than half such subsidiaries.[9]

Once again, these proportions, particularly the second, are smaller than those in Canada. A possible explanation in regard to executives, apart from that of difference in distance, is that the Canadian salary scale and other executive benefits may be closer to the American than those of the United Kingdom or Australia, so that it is somewhat easier to persuade Americans to move to Canada. Since many of the subsidiaries' executives are also on the boards of the subsidiaries, the higher ratio of American executives could also lead to a higher ratio of Americans on the boards in Canada, compared with the other two countries.

Some Implications for Canada

It is our view that Canada has a dual interest in this question of nationals in management and on boards of foreign-owned subsidiary companies. Clearly she must insist that competent Canadians not be prevented from taking senior positions in such firms. It may be suggested that the wide representation of Canadians in the management and on the boards of these companies indicates that discrimination as such cannot be widespread. Obviously, however, there is room for improvement among a significant minority of the firms, particularly in regard to presidents. Furthermore, it may well be that French-speaking Canadians particularly are inadequately represented in the senior management positions and on the boards of foreign-owned subsidiaries, although in this respect such firms appear to have followed the undesirable practices of their Canadian-owned counterparts. At the same time, one must recognize that the utilization of imported personnel and the interest of qualified directors of parent companies, so long as they do not impede the initiatives of the local managers, can do much to improve the performance of the subsidiary firms. It is not evident that the quality of Canadian managerial personnel is so high that Canada's interests would be served by reduced resort to imported persons.

---

[8] *Ibid.*, pp. 105-08, 114. The term American in the data presented by Brash includes all those persons who had been employed for a prolonged period by the U.S. parent.

[9] John H. Dunning, *The Role of American Investment in the British Economy* (London, England: Political and Economic Planning, 1969), Broadsheet 507, p. 128.

Indeed, the Economic Council of Canada has repeatedly drawn attention to the fact that the average educational attainment of the owner and management group in Canada shows a greater shortfall below the average educational attainment of the corresponding group in the United States than is the case with almost any other major category of the labour force. In addition, the pioneering work of John Porter, based mainly on Canadian-owned firms, has suggested that the business élite group in Canada has been extremely narrow in its origins. [10] This point is of some importance, for it may well be that stronger managerial and (partly associated) entrepreneurial capacities drawn more widely and deeply from the various groups in Canada are key elements in any process of successfully repatriating parts of Canadian industry, or of Canadians undertaking a larger proportion of the new ventures than they have undertaken in the past. Closer examination of the quality of management education in Canada, similar to the studies undertaken in the United States in recent years, might well be in order, along with further investigations into problems of entrepreneurship in Canada.

It should be added that managers and directors from outside Canada, often different from Canadians and among themselves in backgrounds and approaches to business problems, have made a significant contribution to Canada in some areas — perhaps particularly because of the rather narrow range from which local business leadership has been drawn. The influence of foreign-owned firms in developing the managerial capacities of Canadians depends, of course, not merely on who the people are who are appointed to key positions, but also on the degree of latitude in decision-making allowed to their managers in Canada.

---

[10] John Porter, *The Vertical Mosaic: An Analysis of Social Class and Power in Canada* (Toronto: University of Toronto Press, 1965). See especially Chaps. 7-9.

3

The Distribution of Powers
Between the Foreign-Owned
Firm and Parent

Apart from contact at the level of the board of the Canadian subsidiary, a very substantial number of contacts exist between officials of the Canadian subsidiary and those of the parent. These consist of representation on the management or executive committee of the subsidiary; informal contacts through visits and correspondence and telephone calls; a variety of written reports; and, occasionally, representation of the officers of the Canadian firm on committees of the parent company. In addition to all this, there is also, of course, considerable technical liaison between the personnel of the affiliated companies. This wide range of contacts serves, among other purposes, to transfer information between the companies and to give the officers of the parent company some idea of the progress of the subsidiary.

The Question of Control

What do all these contacts add up to in terms of the control of the subsidiary's operations by the officers of the parent company? The word "control" is often used in its legal sense to refer to the ultimate powers of the owners of voting stock to determine the policies of the firms they own. But these owners rarely find it necessary to convene a meeting of the board, at which they impose their views through control of stock. How much control is in fact exercised on a continuing basis by officers of the parent over those of the subsidiary? One must admit that rather little is known about this important area of parent-subsidiary relations and that extensive careful work remains to be done before one can speak with confidence about it.

This subject is important because of the effects it may have on other aspects of performance, as well as on management development. Canadian authorities have emphasized the desirability of as much autonomy as possible for the officers of the subsidiary.

One would naturally expect to find a great deal of variation in the degree to which powers are delegated from officers of the parent to those of the subsidiary. On the one hand, there are many factors accounting for tendencies towards the centralizing of decision-making at the parent firm or the review of major decisions of the subsidiaries' officers. For example, there is the need to ensure the consistency of local decisions in relation to the objectives of the over-all firm, and to ensure as great an amount of efficiency, with at least a minimum amount of profit, as is consistent with the other objectives of the firm. There is also the need at times to resolve conflicts of interest between the various companies in an international firm. The development of standardized accounting procedures, improved communications, and the application of the computer may tend to centralize some decisions. Some of the recent literature on international business organization tends to emphasize the forces making for centralization of decision-making.

On the other hand, there are also considerable pressures towards decentralizing at least some of the decisions involved in the subsidiaries' operations. Given the wide differences in the locales of subsidiaries and sometimes in the nature of their operations, some flexibility must be allowed them if they are to be able to compete effectively with other local firms. Moreover, it is not easy to attract and hold competent managers if they are allowed very little scope for decisions. The international firm, like others, must be wary of losing such managers to competitors or to other lines of activity. Also, there is considerable variation in the degree to which subsidiary operations are integrated with those of the parent, and there is considerable variation in the technical aspects of the production and distribution processes. These will call for somewhat different degrees of decentralization of decision-making. The point to be emphasized here is the likelihood of considerable variation in degree in the delegation of powers between different kinds of firms.

Situation in Canada

One extensive survey of this topic for Canada has been made in recent years.[1] That study first takes account of the ultimate legal powers of the owners, their representation on boards of directors, and the close ties between most of the parents and their subsidiaries because of similar technology and products. Within the limits on independent operation imposed by these factors, what is the effective degree of decentralization of responsibility between the parent firms and their Canadian subsidiaries? The author concludes that four distinct types of decentralization are represented:

---

[1] Safarian, *op. cit.*, pp. 78-102.

1. The first major group includes 37 firms (20 percent) which had *"full"* *decentralization* in both operations and policies. In most of these cases, the influence of the parent is exercised directly through only the representation of its own officers on the board of the Canadian company.

2. The second and most important group consists of 111 firms (60 percent) which had a *substantial degree of decentralization* in both operations and policies. Decentralization was qualified by the need to consult the parent company's officers on major changes in policy and on major financial decisions. In many other areas of decision-making, there was a substantial or complete degree of decentralization; these other areas most frequently included production planning, marketing, and labour relations. There was generally a limited degree of decentralization of decisions on new products and techniques. Often the officers of the Canadian company could recommend policy even on major items and on major financial changes, or the decision was made jointly with the officers of the parent company.

3. In the third group, 18 firms (10 percent), there was *considerable operational freedom* within centralized determination of policy.

4. In a fourth group, 19 firms (10 percent), both operations and policies appeared to be *highly centralized.*

The author concluded that, for the four groups taken together, most of the firms enjoyed what Dunning has called "a high degree of controlled autonomy," in the sense that the officers of the subsidiary had operational responsibility and, in most cases, also initiated changes in policy. On the other hand, the officers of the parent had to be consulted on major changes in policy, particularly if these involved financial changes. In addition, the officers of the parent company typically retained the right to appoint the senior executive of the subsidiary.

It should be repeated that these comments on the degree of decentralization refer to firms where ultimate voting power rests with non-residents, where officers of the parent company sit on the boards of the Canadian subsidiaries and exercise an influence in this way, and where there are important ties of a technological and product nature which condition many of the decisions made by the officers of the subsidiary.

While the determinants of the degree of centralization were not exhaustively examined, the author pinpointed several factors as relevant:

1. Subsidiaries that have been established very recently tend to be supervised more closely than older subsidiaries.

2. The existence of a minority share position, if it is closely held, such as by a Canadian company, may reduce the degree of supervision exercised by the parent.

3. Firms that were producing relatively few products, particularly if the products were identical to those of the parent and if there was also a substantial

degree of vertical integration, tended to be more closely supervised.

4.   Firms that were not very profitable or were suffering losses also tended to be closely supervised.

5.   Finally, there appeared to be more supervision where the Canadian subsidiary was the only foreign subsidiary of the parent or was one of a few such subsidiaries.

No doubt there are other factors of importance that a more extensive case-study approach would have unearthed. For example, the parent's attitude towards the degree of decentralization was often important, as was the quality of the local management, although it is not possible to say to what extent these factors work independently of those mentioned above in determining the degree of decentralization of decision-making.

Significance for Canada

The Canadian interest here would appear to be a maximum degree of decentralization of decision-making, consistent with the other objectives of economic and political policy, in order to assure that the interests of the subsidiary are kept to the forefront. The rub occurs in the qualification. Quite clearly, from the standpoint of the international firm, no one degree of decentralization would best suit its purposes at all points of time and at all levels of development of the subsidiary. At the same time it is not clear that maximum decentralization in all cases would suit the best interests of either the subsidiary or Canada, unless Canadians were willing to emphasize this objective regardless of the cost in terms of other objectives. For example, it is well to recognize that the purpose of parental influence in the subsidiary is not simply to exercise centralization of decision-making *per se*, although doubtless, in relationships between different managerial groups, some such factor is often at work. In most cases, a key purpose of centralization is the efficient and profitable functioning of the subsidiary and its rapid growth in the market, or at least its retention of its share of the market relative to other firms. Centralization is thus an aspect of the transfer of techniques to Canada, including managerial techniques.

Suppose a particular subsidiary has run into economic difficulties because of bad management or because of forces beyond its control. It is difficult to see that the interests of Canada would necessarily be best served by allowing the subsidiary to flounder in this unsatisfactory state, at considerable cost to employment and incomes in Canada, rather than by allowing it to have some effective liaison with the officers and other personnel of the parent, if this could be helpful. It may be that the training of managers is enhanced if they can learn to recover from their own mistakes, but presumably there is some limit to the extent to which the community as a whole can be asked to share the losses involved in giving these particular resident managers complete leeway in making and rectifying errors. The essential question in such cases is whether the local managers are in a position to take initiatives, while asking for advice, or are simply told what to do.

It should be emphasized in this context that there are clear limits to the degree to which decentralization of decision-making can be effected. The owners of capital will demand, at the very minimum, some sort of an accounting concerning the use of their assets, with obvious implications for major policies and major finances at least. Put differently, at some point the decentralization of decision-making between firms can go no further without a divorce. At that point the advocacy of further decentralization becomes a case against direct foreign investment as such, and not simply a question regarding the operational results of such companies.

Comparison with Australia and the United Kingdom

It is interesting to compare the degree of control exercised in Canada with the experience of American subsidiaries in Australia. We noted earlier the far smaller proportion of Americans among the senior executive positions of the Australian subsidiaries than in Canada. There also appears to be far less direct contact through visits, given the distance involved, though more reporting perhaps compensates for this. As to the degree of decentralization of decision-making, capital expenditures are (as in Canada) the most carefully controlled item, with product innovation second. Thus 75 subsidiaries (79 percent) reported that they had to seek parent approval on major capital expenditure, while 20 (21 percent) could act independently. The comparable figures in the case of product innovation and development were 58 and 37[2] (61 percent and 39 percent). In production-planning and wages policy and labour relations, 90 percent or more of the firms reported that they could act independently. Brash goes on to note that the initiative for major management decisions, including major capital outlays, in the great majority of firms examined comes from the local management, regardless of where final authority lies. He notes also, however, that it is through the influence of the parent on the decision-making process that the management and other techniques of the parent company are transferred to the subsidiary.[3]

Observing the situation in Britain, Dunning distinguishes three groups in this respect. The first (49 firms or 33 percent of his sample) is strongly controlled in that there is strong influence of the parent executives on decision-making in the subsidiary, and there may also be frequent interchange of personnel, export control, and so on. The second group (59 firms or 39 percent) is partly controlled ("a high degree of controlled autonomy"), in that major decisions involving capital in particular or new product designs must be approved by head office, but the management (usually British) is allowed wide operating freedom within this over-all policy framework. The specialized needs of the subsidiary and the country involved are taken into account, and the local executives exercise much initiative on policy. The third group (42 firms or 28 percent) is negligibly controlled, in that contacts are limited and essentially involve

---

[2] The definition of American investment used by Brash extends to firms with only 25 percent of their capital owned in the United States. The figures of 20 and 37 for independent action given here include 11 and 12, respectively, where American ownership was 25-49 percent of the firm.

[3] Brash, *op. cit.*, pp. 113-28.

exchange of technical information. The subsidiary operates independently as long as its profits are reasonable. Dunning found that wholly owned subsidiaries constituted a larger proportion of group 1 than of the other two groups. The major reason for this was that joint ventures owned by a British and an American firm were more prominent in groups 2 and 3.[4]

---

[4] John H. Dunning, *American Investment in British Manufacturing Industry* (London, England: George Allen and Unwin, 1958), pp. 107-11.

4

The External Trade
of Foreign-Owned Firms

In an examination of the performance of subsidiary companies in Canada, the question of their exports and imports has a natural and prominent place. Many subsidiaries were established in Canada to supply the parent company or other purchasers abroad with raw materials. The establishment of many others, particularly manufacturing companies, was at least partly due to Canadian tariffs, as will be discussed more fully. In the latter circumstances, the parent company, although locating some production facilities in Canada, would tend to supply its subsidiary there with some components and materials, unless the Canadian tariff on these was prohibitive. Most manufacturing subsidiaries are unlikely, in their early stages, to be significant exporters, as witness the fact that they cannot produce in Canada without a tariff to protect them. Some of them, however, will in time develop trade with affiliates or other companies abroad as their cost structures for some products improve and for other reasons. In some cases, an international company chooses to specialize the output of its various subsidiaries from the outset, so that they export and import substantial amounts of manufactured items as a matter of course.

Issue for Canada

The major economic question which has arisen in Canada regarding the foreign trade of subsidiary companies is whether the fact of foreign ownership inhibits exports and stimulates excessive imports, particularly of manufactured products.[1] It is often stated that the very existence of affiliates abroad prevents

---

[1] As elsewhere, questions that arise from the extraterritorial extension of foreign laws and regulations to Canada are postponed to a later section.

21

the Canadian firm from serving their markets, while the parent may insist that the subsidiary purchase from it in order to increase its own sales. This leads to deficits on trade for Canada and less expansion of her manufacturing production than would otherwise be the case.

If a firm is interested in maximizing its profits internationally, it should in principle place its sources of supply, including those for export, in the most efficient locations, whether these are in the domestic market of the parent company or in the domestic market of a subsidiary. From a profit standpoint, it would be irrational for the firm to continue to favour a particular location that was less efficient than others, even though these others may be abroad. The profits, after all, accrue to the parent. Similarly, a resident-owned firm too would be expected to locate where it could operate most efficiently over time, rather than to favour a domestic location simply because it was domestic.

Three exceptions may be suggested to this general principle that economic efficiency of production and distribution determines location over time.

In the short run, during which existing facilities have not yet been written off, the parent firm may attempt to protect them from inroads by affiliated firms, particularly if these facilities have excess capacity. But protection for higher-cost facilities can be presumed, in all logic, to run both ways. In other words, the international firm may give such temporary protection to its facilities in Canada, on occasion, and not only to those located elsewhere. The facilities and the profits, as just noted, belong to the same international firm. It may even be reasonable to suppose that, if Canadian unit costs of production tend in most cases to be higher than those of the parent or other affiliates, the protection may be extended more often to the Canadian subsidiary than to the other parts of the international firm. In any event, this is a short-run consideration only — partly because the firm will write off assets over time or will require new facilities as demand expands, and partly because competitive firms will use the more efficient location and will force the firm in question to do likewise. If the operations are of a type in which technology requires a high concentration of plant, the short run will pertain to a longer period.

The second exception has to do with situations in which competition is restricted by agreement among firms, involving restriction of markets to which firms may ship and restriction in the use of industrial property rights such as patents. We shall return to this topic later in this section.

The third exception has to do with non-economic factors which threaten the value of the asset or the returns to the parent.

Data for Canada

The only comprehensive study of the trade of ˙American subsidiary companies in Canada is the one in the U.S. Department of Commerce census for 1957.[2] All other studies on the subject, including other official studies by

---

[2] U.S. Department of Commerce, *U.S. Business Investments in Foreign Countries*, 1960.

Canadian and American governments, cover only part of the firms involved, usually the major ones. The census for 1957 showed that American-owned enterprises in Canadian manufacturing, mining, and petroleum industries sold $10.7 billion (U.S.) in that year. Of this amount, $1.4 billion (13.1 percent) was exported to the United States and $0.7 billion (6.5 percent) to other countries, so that exports represented 20 percent of total sales. It should be noted that these exports by American subsidiaries in Canada represented about half of all Canadian exports of manufactures (including pulp and paper) in that year, and they also represented more than 85 percent of exports of petroleum and other minerals and metals combined. These proportions are *higher* than those representing the American ownership of capital invested in these Canadian industries during that year. Residents of the United States owned 39 percent and controlled 43 percent of the capital of Canadian manufacturing industries at the end of 1957, and 53 percent and 63 percent of the combined capital in petroleum and mining industries. In other words, on an over-all basis, American direct investment firms in Canada exported more than their share of total exports, to judge by these data.[3]

Unfortunately, this was the last such comprehensive census that the U.S. government has published to date.[4] More-recent annual data rely on samples based on the major companies only, which are used to estimate the over-all totals. They include only manufacturing and mining and specifically exclude petroleum, which has become an important export industry in Canada. These data (see Tables 3 and 4) show that American direct investment firms in manufacturing industries in Canada exported almost 20 percent of their total sales in 1965 ($2,537 million of $13,445 million). In the same year, European affiliates of American firms exported somewhat over 20 percent of their total sales. Latin American affiliates exported less than 10 percent, as did affiliates in all other geographic areas — i.e., in Africa, Asia, and Oceania. Table 4 shows considerable variation by country in the percentage of the total sales of American subsidiaries which went to exports (see column 3). It is worth noting that, in 1965, American affiliates in Canadian manufacturing industries accounted for 48 percent of exports of manufactures from Canada, while at the end of 1963 (the last year for which data are available) residents of the United States owned 44 percent and controlled 46 percent of the capital invested in Canadian manufacturing. In the United Kingdom, on the other hand, American direct investment companies would seem to be even more export-oriented, since they accounted for 17 percent of exports of manufactures while accounting for about 7½ percent of the capital and about 10 percent of the sales of British manufacturing industries.

It is important to add that the exports are concentrated among certain kinds of products. Table 5 gives industry-group details of exports by American manufacturing affiliates in Canada and elsewhere, highlighting the differences between Canada and other countries in the percentage of exports to sales for

---

[3] Safarian, *op. cit.*, pp. 119-20, estimated from data published by the U.S. Department of Commerce and the Dominion Bureau of Statistics.

[4] A similar census for 1966 is under preparation and will be released, it is hoped, before 1970.

TABLE 3

LOCAL SALES AND EXPORTS BY U.S. DIRECT INVESTMENT
MANUFACTURING AND MINING COMPANIES IN VARIOUS AREAS, 1965
(millions of U.S. dollars)

Area	U.S. Manufacturing Affiliates				U.S. Mining Affiliates			
	All Sales	Local Sales	All Exports	Exports to U.S.	All Sales	Local Sales	All Exports	Exports to U.S.
All areas	42,377	34,693	7,684	1,856	3,426	784	2,642	1,225
Canada	13,445	10,908	2,537	1,458	1,400	395	1,005	607
Latin America	5,484	5,073	411	101	1,345	240	1,105	535
Europe	18,761	14,357	4,404	220	60	10	50	1
Other areas	4,687	4,355	332	77	621	139	482	82

Source: U.S. Department of Commerce, *Survey of Current Business*, November, 1966.

TABLE 4

TOTAL SALES AND EXPORT SALES OF U.S. MANUFACTURING AFFILIATES
AND COUNTRY'S TOTAL EXPORTS OF MANUFACTURES,
SELECTED COUNTRIES, 1965
(millions of U.S. dollars)

Country	(1) U.S. Affiliates Total Sales	(2) Exports	(3) Ratio (2) to (1) (%)	(4) Country's Exports of Manufactures	(5) Ratio (2) to (4) (%)
Canada	13,445	2,537	19	5,280[a]	48
Belgium, Netherlands, Luxembourg	1,589	557	35	8,860	6
France	2,665	440	17	7,330	6
Germany	4,356	1,160	27	15,920	7
Italy	1,272	184	14	5,610	3
United Kingdom	7,510	1,887	25	11,180	17
Japan	920	72	8	7,830	1

[a]Adjusted to include newsprint, paper and pulp, and pelletized iron ore, to provide comparability with statistics on sales of manufacturing affiliates.

Source: U.S. Department of Commerce, *Survey of Current Business,* November, 1966.

TABLE 5

EXPORTS AS A PERCENTAGE OF SALES,
FOREIGN MANUFACTURING AFFILIATES OF U.S. COMPANIES,
BY INDUSTRY GROUP AND GEOGRAPHIC AREA, 1965
(percentages)

Industry Group	All Areas	Canada	Latin America[a]	Europe	Other
Food products	13.2	10.0	22.3	7.7	27.1
Paper and allied products	47.2	60.0	11.2	8.4	4.6
Chemicals	15.8	11.5	9.9	24.2	8.6
Rubber products	8.5	1.9	0.6	21.8	4.5
Primary and fabricated metals	25.2	38.7	3.9	18.5	2.7
Machinery, excluding electrical	22.7	12.8	6.2	31.5	5.0
Electrical machinery	11.6	7.5	1.5	15.9	10.0
Transportation equipment	16.5	11.3	0.7	26.7	3.8
Other products	17.0	12.9	3.0	26.2	4.7
All commodities	18.1	18.9	7.5	23.5	7.1

[a]Includes "other western hemisphere."

Source: U.S. Department of Commerce, *Survey of Current Business,* November 1966,
          p. 9.

various kinds of products. In paper and allied products and in primary and fabricated metals, the Canadian export percentage greatly exceeds that for other regions, reflecting Canada's comparative advantage in these industries. In non-electrical machinery, the Canadian export percentage is much below that of other developed areas as a whole. For most manufactured products, Canadian export percentages tend to be below those of Europe and above those for other areas. The discrepancy between Canada and Europe is large in non-electrical machinery, transportation equipment, rubber products, and chemicals. The point to be emphasized is that American subsidiaries in Europe export large portions of their output of manufactured products — in the range of 16 percent to 32 percent. Apparently American direct investment in a country's manufacturing industry is no bar to substantial exports of manufactures if the costs of production and distribution, the associated research base, and related circumstances warrant. It should be added also that about 60 percent of exports of manufactures by Canadian subsidiaries went to the United States, in contrast with much smaller proportions for exports by American manufacturing affiliates in other parts of the world.

Data are also available on the sales of American mining affiliates located in foreign countries. They indicate that for each of the major direct investment regions — namely, Canada, Latin America, Europe, and other areas — at least 70 percent of sales of mining products are for export.

Turning now to the imports of subsidiaries in Canada, we find that the U.S. census of 1957 was unable to estimate a total for such trade. We must therefore rely on the subsequent annual estimates, which are based on a survey of the larger companies that is then blown up to an over-all estimate for all companies. Moreover, no data are available on the imports of mining and petroleum affiliates in Canada of American companies, although such firms are known to have a much smaller propensity to import than manufacturing firms. All in all, then, we are restricted to the annual estimates by the U.S. Department of Commerce of the imports from the United States into Canada by only the manufacturing affiliates of American firms.

As Table 6 shows, these affiliates imported $1,840 million of goods into Canada from the United States in 1964. The major categories were $628 million for processing or assembly from parent firms, almost all of which was parts, components, and similar manufactures; $659 million from parent firms for resale without further manufacture; and $438 million of imports purchased directly by the affiliates from other sources in the United States. Such imports to Canada are highly concentrated in a few industry groups, as witness the fact that fully $651 million was imported by the transportation equipment industry in Canada, $331 million by the non-electrical machinery industry, $245 million by electrical machinery industries, and $207 million by chemical industries. It is also worth noting that such imports into Canada, as a percentage of the sales of the Canadian subsidiaries, were as high as 25.7 percent in the case of transportation equipment and 29.5 percent in the case of non-electrical machinery. Furthermore, in total and in most of the particular industrial categories, such imports as a percentage of the sales of the subsidiary companies were higher for Canada than for other areas in which American affiliates are located.[5]

TABLE 6

U.S. EXPORTS TO FOREIGN-PRODUCTION AFFILIATES OF U.S. MANUFACTURING FIRMS BY INDUSTRY OF AFFILIATES AND BY TYPE OF EXPORTS, 1964

	Exports to Affiliates (millions of U.S. dollars)		Exports to Affiliates as % of Their Sales[a]	
	All Areas	Canada	All Areas	Canada
Industry of Foreign Affiliates				
Food products	165	53	3.3	4.1
Paper and allied products	57	27	2.9	2.2
Chemicals	638	207	8.4	11.7
Rubber products	156	46	8.2	9.5
Primary and fabricated metals	189	74	5.2	5.1
Machinery (except electrical)	730	331	14.1	29.5
Electrical machinery	357	245	10.4	23.0
Transportation equipment	1,293	651	12.7	25.7
Other products	484	205	11.2	16.1
Total	4,068	1,840	9.6	15.1
Type of Exports				
Charged on parent company books:				
For processing or assembly	1,589	628		
For resale without further manufacture	1,403	659		
Capital equipment	198	56		
Other exports charged to parent	24	8		
Exports purchased in United States directly by foreign affiliate	578	438		
Exports sold by affiliate for commission	275	50		

[a]Excludes exports of capital equipment for use by foreign affiliates ($198 million) and exports for sale by the foreign affiliate on a commission basis ($275 million).

Source: U.S. Department of Commerce, *Survey of Current Business,* December, 1965, pp. 15-16.

We will note here and below that the largest import figure to Canada in absolute terms, and one of the largest relative to sales, is for transportation

---

[5] This may be due, in part, to the uneven quality of the data reported by countries. In the study for 1963, about two-thirds of all purchases made directly in the United States by the foreign affiliates (rather than by or through the parent) were allocated to Canadian affiliates. The source notes that "it is not known yet whether such direct purchases in the United States by affiliates in other countries are in fact quite small, or whether the records of the parent companies do not reflect them." *Survey of Current Business*, December, 1964, p. 22.

equipment. Most of this represents automobiles and parts. In this case there has been a substantial change since the period 1964-65 to which these data apply, as a result of the Canada-U.S. automotive agreement of 1965. Specifically, there has been a substantial reduction in the Canadian deficit on automobiles and parts. The data below for the total trade in automobiles and parts between the two countries suggest the extent of the changes in recent years:

CANADIAN - U.S. AUTOMOTIVE TRADE [6]
(millions of U.S. dollars)

	1964	1965	1966	1967	1968p
Canadian Statistics					
U.S. to Canada	659	929	1,416	2,001	2,744
Canada to U.S.	90	213	780	1,465	2,260
U.S. Trade Surplus	569	716	636	536	484
U.S. Statistics					
U.S. to Canada	654	860	1,311	1,801	2,421
Canada to U.S.	76	247	889	1,562	2,580
U.S. Trade Surplus	578	613	422	239	-159

p = preliminary

It is not possible to estimate the foreign trade balance of U.S. subsidiaries in Canada from data published by the U.S. Department of Commerce. For one thing, country data on the petroleum industry are excluded from its estimates. In addition, this source gives no over-all figure for the total imports of American mining and manufacturing affiliates in Canada, although indicating that the manufacturing affiliates alone have a substantial deficit in trade with the United States. This is hardly a measure of the total trade of these manufacturing subsidiaries, because they export and import substantial amounts to and from overseas countries. Moreover, the mining affiliates in Canada appear to be substantial net exporters.

Industry Distribution of Foreign Trade

For a more detailed look at the industrial composition of exports and imports of subsidiary companies in Canada (not restricted to those with U.S. parents or to trade with the United States), one can turn to the report published in 1967 by the Canadian Department of Trade and Commerce and the Dominion

---

[6] Source: Official statistics of each country as given in the second and third editions of the *Annual Report of the President to the Congress on the Operation of the Automotive Products Trade Act of 1965*, Washington, 1968 and 1969. The growing discrepancies between U.S. and Canadian data reflect differences in valuing vehicles, classifying parts, and recording transfers of certain tools and charges for engineering services. Both governments are working on ways to produce more-comparable data for their automotive trade.

Bureau of Statistics, entitled *Foreign-Owned Subsidiaries in Canada*. These figures are summarized in Table 7. Unlike the preceding case, no attempt was made to blow up these data — which are for a sample of 266 companies, each with assets in excess of $5 million — to over-all figures for all foreign-owned companies in Canada. In addition, there are two important points to note about the nature of the foreign trade statistics in the report we are discussing. As the report itself points out on page 9, its import figures generally include duties and transportation charges within Canada. In other words, the import values are mainly c.i.f., which is a very different basis from that of the import data for Canada compiled by the Dominion Bureau of Statistics and from that of the American export series just discussed, both of which are on an f.o.b. basis and thus exclude such transfer costs. In fact, the duties and transportation charges within Canada are not international transactions, since they are payable to Canadian recipients. Thus the import figures in Table 7 are inflated by some significant but unknown amount, a fact which must affect our interpretation of them. The second qualification is that, since the report classifies exports according to final seller, a significant volume of grain exports is classified to foreign-owned subsidiaries in the wholesale trade. If an adjustment were made for this, it would reduce or eliminate the Canadian trade surplus, while removal of the overvaluation of imports would work in the opposite direction.

This study suggests that these 266 foreign-owned companies alone accounted for at least one-third of all Canadian exports and about the same proportion of all imports. About 20 percent of their sales in 1964 and 1965 were abroad, and about 30 percent of their purchases of goods were from

TABLE 7

SOURCES OF IMPORTS AND DESTINATION OF EXPORTS OF
LARGER DIRECT INVESTMENT COMPANIES IN CANADA, 1965
(millions of Canadian dollars)

	With the United States	With Other Countries	Total
Total trade of these subsidiaries:			
Exports from Canada	1,732.5	1,013.4	2,745.9
Imports into Canada	2,077.6	605.3	2,682.9
Balance	- 345.1	408.1	63.0
Trade with parent and affiliates abroad:			
Exports from Canada	1,094.0	299.2	1,393.2
Imports into Canada	1,481.1	446.8	1,927.9
Balance	- 387.1	- 147.6	- 534.7
Trade with non-affiliates:			
Exports from Canada	638.5	714.2	1,352.7
Imports into Canada	596.6	158.5	755.1
Balance	41.9	555.7	597.6

Source: Department of Trade and Commerce, *Foreign-Owned Subsidiaries in Canada*, pp. 11-12.

abroad. In both 1964 and 1965 the value of exports of these 266 firms exceeded the value of their imports. In 1964 exports and imports were $2.53 billion and $2.20 billion, respectively, while in 1965 exports were $2.75 billion and imports were $2.68 billion. The trade surpluses of $333.5 million in 1964 and $63.0 million in 1965 reflect deficits with the United States offset by surpluses with other foreign countries. Further, the international transactions of the subsidiary companies were largely concentrated in the United States. In 1965 fully 63 percent of all exports ($1.73 billion of $2.75 billion) went to that market, and 78 percent of all foreign purchases ($2.08 billion of $2.68 billion) came from that country. The subsidiary companies' foreign markets and sources of supply are particularly concentrated with the parents and affiliates abroad. In 1965 about 50 percent of all foreign sales ($1.39 billion of $2.75 billion) were to such affiliates, and 72 percent of all purchases abroad ($1.93 billion of $2.68 billion) came from such affiliates. In 1965 the 266 companies had a deficit of $345 million in trade with the United States and a deficit of over $500 million in trade with their affiliates.

Canadian data on the industrial distribution of foreign trade of subsidiary companies in 1965 (Table 8) confirm that the deficit is highly concentrated by industry. Specifically, there was a deficit of $610 million in trade in transportation equipment (mainly automobiles and parts) alone. There was also a deficit of $175 million in machinery and metal-fabricating. All other cases of deficits were under $100 million each. Substantial surpluses were recorded in pulp and paper ($700 million), mining and primary metals ($289.4 million), and whole-

TABLE 8

COMMODITY EXPORTS AND IMPORTS OF LARGER FOREIGN-OWNED
SUBSIDIARIES IN CANADA, BY INDUSTRY, 1965

	Exports	Imports[a]	Balance	Exports as % of Sales	Imports as % of Purchases
	(millions of Canadian dollars)				
Mining and primary metals	356.8	67.4	289.4	52.1	22.1
Gas and oil	294.0	355.7	- 61.7	10.3	24.1
Machinery and metal-fabricating	93.9	268.9	-175.0	8.4	41.1
Transportation equipment	401.1	1,010.5	-609.5	12.7	54.1
Electrical products	99.6	162.8	- 63.2	9.7	29.5
Chemical products	103.8	185.6	- 81.8	9.8	31.0
Food and beverages	117.6	169.1	- 51.5	8.2	19.0
Pulp and paper	731.8	32.0	699.9	65.3	6.8
Other manufacturing	73.7	171.5	- 97.8	7.5	32.8
Wholesale trade	463.7	200.4	263.3	56.7	26.2
Other industries	9.9	59.1	- 49.2	1.1	10.2
Total	2,745.9	2,683.0	63.0	18.2	30.9

[a]Includes purchases of capital equipment.

Source: Department of Trade and Commerce, *Foreign-Owned Subsidiaries in Canada,*
           pp. 12 and 14.

sale trade ($263.3 million). What stands out from these 1965 data is the export orientation of industries that have a strong natural resource base, whether the products are exported in primary or processed state; the huge deficit in transportation equipment industries in particular, a deficit which is being reduced as a result of the automobile arrangements with the United States; and a considerable variety in experience by various types of industries.

It is worth noting the proportions of exports to total sales and of imports to total purchases by Canadian subsidiaries within these industrial groups in 1965. The two right-hand columns of Table 8 confirm that the major exporters relative to total sales were pulp and paper and mining and primary metals (if we overlook wholesale trade, which is a distributing industry). Most other industry groups exported between 8 and 13 percent of their sales. On the import side, transportation equipment stood out by itself, since imports ran as high as 54 percent in relation to purchases. The machinery and metal-fabricating industry also showed a relatively high ratio of imports to total purchases. These proportions reflect imports of commodities as a percentage of purchases of commodities; the domestic content for these industries, when labour is taken into account, would be significantly higher than the figures shown. The data by industry can be summarized by noting that the natural-resource-oriented industries accounted for $1.85 billion of exports in 1965, or two-thirds of all foreign sales by reporting companies. Imports by these resource-oriented industries amounted to only $655 million, so that there was a favourable trade balance of about $1.2 billion. By contrast, other industries accounted for imports of $2.0 billion and exports of about $900 million, for a $1.1 billion deficit.

The data compiled separately by Safarian on the export pattern of subsidiaries in Canada extend these findings somewhat. His data concentrate on the *numbers* of firms falling into certain export categories, rather than on the over-all *value* of their exports, thus giving a clearer indication of the typical performance of the direct investment company. Almost half the 280 foreign-owned firms in his study did not export in 1959 or in the late fifties; in one-quarter of the group, exports were 5 or less percent of their sales; and in the remaining quarter, exports were over 5 percent. By far the most common destination of exports was the United States. Almost half the firms with exports sent 70 percent or more of them to the United States. Roughly the same was true for American-owned firms taken by themselves. In other words, even for the American-owned firms, the most likely export destination was the country in which the parent was located. At the same time, the most likely export destination for the particular firms he was studying was not to affiliates abroad, whether in the United States or elsewhere. Fully 62 percent of the firms with exports sent 70 percent or more of their exports to non-affiliated entities. At the same time, the parent company and other affiliates abroad were a very important market for those Canadian subsidiaries with exports, as witnessed by the fact that almost half reported some exports to the parent and over one-fourth of those with exports sold over 30 percent of their exports to the parent. A smaller portion was also sold to affiliates of the parent. Only 34 percent and 40 percent of those with exports had some exports to the United Kingdom and to other sterling-area countries, respectively.

Safarian's data show a substantial increase in exports as a percentage of sales as the size of the firm grows, with all the firms with assets of over $25 million showing exports, while 72 percent of the firms with assets of under $1 million had no exports. The industries oriented to primary resources reported much larger shares of their output being sold abroad than did secondary manufacturing. The data also show that firms in Canada whose products were identical with those of the parent generally exported a smaller share of their output than did those whose products were modified. (Subsidiaries whose products were not comparable to those of the parent—such firms were found most commonly in the extractive industries — export a substantial portion of their output, as already noted.) Moreover, as the range of the subsidiaries' products compared with that of the parent narrowed, the firms tended to be more oriented to exports.

To turn to the import content of the subsidiaries' production, it is well to note, first, that this is likely to be substantial. Many of these companies begin their existence as a partial alternative to imports into Canada. Moreover, the similarity of products between parent and subsidiary will reinforce the tendency to import from the parent or from its sources of supply. At the same time it is a very common experience for firms gradually to raise their domestic content once they are established in the domestic environment. Sometimes differences in the requirements of the Canadian market will reinforce the process whereby costs of transfer to Canada (including the Canadian tariff) and the economies of decentralization of production and distribution lead to increases in domestic content.

Safarian's data show that roughly one-third of the firms purchased 90 percent or more of their components, materials, and services from Canadian sources; another third purchased between 70 percent and 89 percent from such sources; and the remaining third, less than 70 percent. For the group in general, imports were largely from the United States, with about 74 percent of the firms indicating that they took 70 percent or more of their imports from that country. About 60 percent bought nothing from the United Kingdom. The parent firms abroad are the major source of subsidiary imports into Canada. Even for firms owned overseas (i.e., elsewhere than in the United States), imports into Canada from the United States typically run almost as large as such imports from overseas. Curiously enough, in spite of Commonwealth preferences, none of the firms owned overseas bought imports from sterling-area countries other than the United Kingdom, and only 7 percent of the American-owned firms bought anything at all from such sources. The percentage of purchases from suppliers in Canada is higher for the larger firms than for the smaller ones. The age of the firm has an effect on domestic content only for firms that have a very large import content in their supplies. In other words, apart from certain *minima* due probably to the nature of production and the tariff, there does not appear to be much relationship between the age of the firm and domestic content. The data confirm the conclusion noted earlier, that the industries oriented to primary resources have a very high Canadian content in their purchases, while industries

TABLE 9

PERCENTAGE OF SALES AND PURCHASES IN CANADA, RESIDENT- AND NON-RESIDENT-OWNED COMPANIES WITH ASSETS OF $1 MILLION OR MORE, 1959[a]

Percentage of Sales in Canada	All Firms R	NR	Assets of $25 Million or More R	NR	Percentage of Purchases in Canada	All Firms R	NR	Assets of $25 Million or More R	NR
100%	30	31	40	0	95% and over	36	11	40	11
95 - 99	30	37	10	43	90 - 94	14	18	20	17
90 - 94	3	8	5	9	80 - 89	19	18	20	17
80 - 89	3	7	5	6	70 - 79	7	14	0	14
70 - 79	4	3	15	6	60 - 69	6	10	5	14
50 - 69	3	1		0	50 - 59	3	4	0	3
Below 50	18	7	20	26	40 - 49	1	4	0	3
No reply	5	6	5	11	30 - 39	0	4	0	0
					Below 30	2	4	0	0
					No reply	12	13	15	20
Total	100	100	100	100	Total	100	100	100	100
Total number	96	160	20	35		96	160	20	35

AVERAGES FOR ABOVE DATA
(percentages)

Percentage of Sales in Canada	All Types of Business R	NR	Manufacturing Only R	NR
First quartile	100	100	100	100
Median	99	98	99	99
Third quartile	75	90	93	95

Percentage of Purchases in Canada	All Types of Business R	NR	Manufacturing Only R	NR
First quartile	96	90	95	90
Median	90	80	90	80
Third quartile	80	64	75	65

[a] Or average of late fifties where 1959 was not typical.
Note: R means resident-owned, NR means non-resident-owned.
Source: A.E. Safarian, Foreign Ownership of Canadian Industry, pp. 274 and 277.

CHART 2

PROPORTION OF SALES AND PURCHASES IN CANADA,
RESIDENT- AND NON-RESIDENT-OWNED COMPANIES
WITH ASSETS OF $1 MILLION OR MORE, 1959

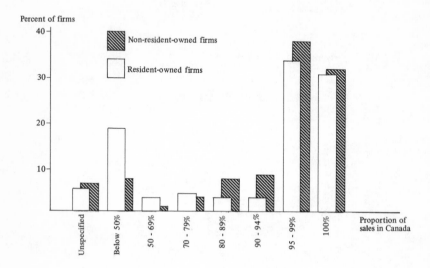

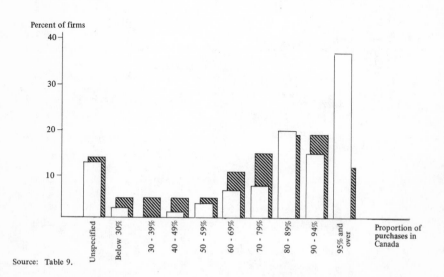

Source: Table 9.

such as transportation equipment and electrical products, representing highly manufactured products, generally tend to have a significantly lower domestic content in purchases. Moreover, those firms which produce a minority, or only a few, of the parent's products have a higher domestic content in their purchases than do those producing a much wider range of products relative to the parent's.[7]

Effects of Foreign Ownership

These absolute figures do not answer directly the question of the effect of foreign ownership on exports and imports. This topic has been studied by Safarian by means of questionnaires and interviews. His findings can be summarized as follows: In the first place, it is often suggested that it is the existence of competing assets abroad that inhibits exports of subsidiary companies. This proposition was tested by the use of data on exports and on the number of affiliates abroad for 238 of the 280 firms in his study. It should be noted that variables other than the number of affiliates abroad will affect exports. Allowance was made for one of these variables by examining data within three size categories of firms, but allowance could not be made for other variables. This test indicated that there was no tendency for firms to export less as the number of their affiliates abroad increased. On the contrary, there was the opposite tendency.[8] More directly, the firms were asked to indicate in what ways affiliation had affected the volume, nature, and direction of their exports. In almost two-thirds of the replies, it appears that affiliation had little or no effect on exports (for example, because transfer costs were prohibitive) or that the question was not applicable (for example, because the company had just been established). In 39 cases the reply was that the effect of affiliation was favourable for reasons that included obtaining contacts with customers abroad, securing guaranteed purchases by affiliates, and using the name, the research, or the sales organization of the parent. On the other hand, 20 firms stated that the effect of affiliation was unfavourable because the firms were restricted in their exports to specific countries or because exports had been reduced or could not be undertaken, owing to the existence of affiliates abroad. In some of these latter cases, the subsidiary's affiliates abroad had lower costs than itself, so that it is not clear that exports could have been made if the subsidiary had been an independent firm and if its cost structure was unchanged. These findings, of course, relate to the *direct* effects on exports as seen by the officers of the subsidiaries.

The author goes on to note, however, that there are two other problems associated with the exports of some Canadian subsidiaries. In the first place, a number of them export through the parent's export sales organization. In many cases this is an aid to exports, but in some cases the method of allocating exports among the parent and the various subsidiaries limits exports because the subsidiaries are not permitted to bid on existing export orders or to solicit new export business on their own.

---

[7] Safarian, *op. cit.*, pp. 121-27, 151-55.
[8] *Ibid.*, p. 128.

The second problem is the allocation of industrial property rights, such as patents, within the international firm. Very often this carries a market restriction in that the subsidiary has the patent for only its own market or for only its own and some specified foreign markets. It should be added that the usual point of such a restriction is not to prevent exports by an efficient subsidiary, for such exports would benefit the parent company through increased profits. The typical reason is to prevent third parties from interfering with the sales of the parent and of its subsidiaries. However, the parent company is often in the position of having granted exclusive marketing rights to particular national markets not only to other subsidiaries, but to non-affiliated companies. Thus, when one of the subsidiaries is potentially able to enter the foreign market efficiently, it may find that it does not have such rights under its patent. We should also note that the effect of the exclusive granting of the Canadian market to the subsidiary is to prevent imports of the patented product into its market by both related and unrelated parties. It will be recognized that the issues noted here are more directly concerned with the characteristics of the international patent system than with simply the question of foreign ownership. This point may be emphasized by noting that many Canadian-owned firms that have made licensing agreements with foreign firms are also restricted to the Canadian market insofar as the sales rights for these products are concerned. Indeed, licensing arrangements between unrelated parties would appear to be even more restrictive as to marketing rights than licensing arrangements between related parties.[9]

Finally an attempt was made to gain some idea of the over-all importance of different kinds of private trade restrictions by bringing together cases where the patent rights apply to Canada only, where the affiliation was stated to be unfavourable with regard to exports, and where those subsidiaries which exported through the parent firm could not bid on exports. The conclusion was that about 15 percent of the firms were subject to private trade restrictions of the kinds noted. These were highly concentrated in the machinery industries, electrical-products industries, and in some branches of the chemical industries. In most cases these restrictions are potential rather than actual, since the great majority of them apply to subsidiaries whose unit costs of production exceed those of their foreign affiliates.[10] In other words, the restrictions may reflect, rather than affect, competitive advantage. Nevertheless, it is difficult to say how much Canadian competitive advantage itself would be improved *because* of any exports accruing in the absence of such restrictions. In any case, where Canadian production costs fall relative to other countries and where other barriers to trade are reduced (such as trade restrictions and distribution costs), these private trade restrictions will become a more important impediment to exports.

The only other available study of export franchises of direct investment firms is that for Australia. It includes both direct investment companies and those with an overseas licensing agreement. It showed that about 275 of the 650 Australian firms thus associated with American firms (42 percent) had an interest in exports. About 100 of these (15 percent of the 650) had no export

---

[9] *Ibid.*, pp. 142 and 285.
[10] *Ibid.*, pp. 142-43.

franchise or one that was restricted. The survey did not ascertain the export interest of the 500 firms associated with British firms, but about 70 had a restricted export franchise. This study must be qualified by the fact that subsidiaries are likely to have a broader export franchise than independent firms with a licensing agreement and by the fact that the franchises of firms without an export interest are not known.[11]

The same questions can be raised regarding imports. Half of the 192 Canadian subsidiaries from which information was received on this point believed affiliation had no *direct* effect on their imports, or a limited one at most. This must be qualified, as noted earlier, by the fact that indirect effects of affiliation are often significant. For example, similarity of products produced by the two firms leads to substantial imports of parts. Forty firms (21 percent) indicated the direct effects included joint purchases with the parent, contacts with suppliers, and other effects, all of which were described as helpful to the subsidiary. Eleven firms (6 percent) reported tied arrangements of various kinds, such as required purchases of parts from the parent or its affiliates. Thirty-four firms (18 percent) indicated affiliation meant large purchases from the parent, although half of these explicitly stated they could buy elsewhere if they wished.[12]

It is not possible to determine from this the precise extent to which tied purchases exist, although it is clear they exist in a minority of the cases. As with export restriction, it must be noted that such restrictions on sources of purchases are likely to be short run at most, since the development of more efficient sources of supply benefits the parent as well as the subsidiary, and that the firms are likely to use or develop such supplies sooner if the pressure of competition is greater. As with exports, such limitations on the ability of the subsidiary to buy in, or develop, the lowest-cost source reduce the welfare both of the subsidiary and of the economy in which it is located. Such intrafirm monopoly, extending across national borders, is a legitimate concern of the national authorities of the country of the subsidiary.

A more direct approach to the question of how nationality of ownership affects performance in foreign trade can be made as follows: The 280 foreign-owned firms in the study were grouped by the degree of foreign ownership — i.e., those whose voting stock was wholly owned abroad, those where there was a minority interest of up to 25 percent, and those with a minority interest of over 25 percent. There turned out to be no statistically significant difference in exports or imports among these ownership groups. [13] The voting stock of all these firms is controlled by non-residents, however, although in varying degrees.

A still more direct test of how ownership affects performance was made by comparing 160 of the non-resident-owned firms and 96 resident-owned firms

---

[11] H. W. Arndt and D. R. Sherk, "Export Franchises of Australian Companies with Overseas Affiliations," *The Economic Record*, August, 1959, pp. 239-42.

[12] Safarian, *op. cit.*, pp. 161-66.

[13] *Ibid.*, p. 259.

with assets of $1 million or more in industries where both types of firm exist. (See Table 9.) No close comparability of products can be claimed, since large, multi-plant firms differ so much, but a broad comparability of size and of industry subgroup permits a test of the effects of ownership on performance. The resident-owned firms were typically older than the non-resident-owned firms and somewhat more heavily representative of extractive industries, but were about the same over-all in distribution of asset size. There is considerable similarity in the foreign trade of these two sets of firms. In each group about 30 percent sell only in Canada; about 33 percent sell up to 5 percent of sales abroad; and the remainder sell over 5 percent of sales abroad. If one looks only at firms with assets of $25 million or more, there is a significant difference in that all the non-resident-owned firms sell something abroad, but 40 percent of the resident-owned do not export. The fact that a larger proportion of the resident-owned firms is in extractive industries can affect these results. But an examination of the 66 resident-owned and 107 non-resident-owned firms which were producing fully processed or manufactured products again revealed that there was not a statistically significant difference in their export performances. The market of the two sets of firms was mainly the United States, and to just about the same extent.

Turning to imports, the two sets of firms differ in that the resident-owned firms in general concentrated more of their purchases in Canada. Thus 36 percent of them bought 95 percent or more of their materials and parts, equipment, and services such as insurance, advertising, and accounting in Canada, as against 11 percent of the non-resident-owned firms. Similar proportions of these firms — 33 percent and 36 percent, respectively — made 80 percent to 94 percent of their purchases in Canada, while a correspondingly greater proportion of the non-resident-owned firms made less than 80 percent of their purchases in Canada. The greater openness of the non-resident-owned firms in this respect persists whether one looks at all firms with assets of $1 million or more, only those with assets of $25 million or more, only those producing fully processed or manufactured products, and once allowance is made for the greater age of the resident-owned firms. A test indicated the difference in import performance was statistically significant. Finally, both groups of firms tended to buy from the same geographic sources — almost three-quarters in each case secured 70 percent or more of their imports from the United States.[14]

The foreign-owned subsidiary in Canada is more import-oriented, in part because it can specialize its output and purchases with respect to those of its parent and other foreign affiliates. Its greater import orientation also reflects the fact that most such firms in Canada were established in part in response to Canadian tariffs. These had the intended effect of leading to local production in place of import of the product; but where the Canadian tariff was not prohibitive, significant imports of the parts and supplies might be expected to continue for such import-competing products. While noting this difference in

---

[14] *Ibid.*, pp. 273, 294-95. Bruce W. Wilkinson has reached similar conclusions on the over-all effects of foreign ownership on exports and imports and has fully analyzed the reasons. See his *Canada's International Trade: An Analysis of Recent Trends and Patterns* (Montreal: Canadian Trade Committee, 1968).

import orientation of the two sets of firms, one should note also the very large extent to which the non-resident-owned firm has substituted local production for imports. The data presented on domestic content, while not a measure of such substitution, suggest this point. An important question indeed is how far this substitution has been done efficiently, a question which will be raised again when the efficiency of subsidiary firms is examined.

Experience of Australia and the United Kingdom

Turning to Australian experience with direct investment companies and their exports, Brash notes that the 93 companies examined had manufactured exports amounting to 2.3 percent of their sales in 1961-62. The U.S. Department of Commerce indicated that exports by American direct investment companies in Australian manufacturing in 1957 amounted to 5.3 percent of their sales. Only eight companies sold 10 percent or more of their sales volume overseas in Brash's list, and the exports of only one of these exceeded 20 percent of total sales.

This export performance is clearly not as good as that of American subsidiaries in Canada nor, as noted below, of those in the United Kingdom. Brash suggests that the reason for this poor performance may be, in part, that Australian manufacturing industry as a whole is not particularly oriented to export. He notes, for example, that the exports of the 93 companies he examined were a higher proportion of total manufactured exports in 1961-62 (10.2 percent) than was the ratio of their manufacturing production to total Australian manufacturing production in that year (6.5 percent), though the measure may overstate the difference involved. He adds that it is not surprising that many of the American-affiliated firms export relatively little, since many of them were set up in Australia largely to surmount trade barriers. The need for the tariff in itself would indicate that their operations were not competitive by world standards, at least initially.

The most frequent reason given by the exporting companies for their relatively small export volume was the high cost of Australian production. A significant proportion of the American affiliates had a limited export franchise as well, although Brash notes that market allocation by the American company often simply recognized the inability of the Australian company to compete abroad. He also notes that the median ratio of exports to sales of the companies which had no limitation on exports was not much higher than the median for the group as a whole. Nevertheless, in the absence of such parental restrictions, a number of companies could have exported a larger proportion of their output, if only because they would be in a better position to reduce their unit cost thereby. It also appears, as in the Canadian experience, that a significantly higher fraction of independent licencees than of financial affiliates were confined to Australia in their sales. Brash adds that foreign affiliation often aids the exports of the subsidiary companies. For example, of the eight companies which had been completely owned by Australians and which gave data on exports before and after the acquisition by an American interest, the exports of seven were higher (in some cases much higher) after the American investment than before it.

Finally, he finds that there has been a considerable expansion of the exports of many American-affiliated companies in recent years, partly because of government tax incentives, partly because the government has prevailed on some companies to relax the export franchises available to the subsidiaries, and partly also because of reduction in Australian unit costs.[15]

Turning to imports by Australian affiliates of American companies, Brash secured information from 77 companies for 1961-62 which indicated that total imports of raw materials, components, and finished goods for resale without further processing amounted to nearly 19 percent of the total sales of the companies concerned. While no strictly comparable Canadian figure is available because of differences in the size of the companies and the items covered, it will be noted that this proportion is considerably less than that reported by the Department of Trade and Commerce for the larger Canadian subsidiaries in 1965 as presented earlier. Brash points out that the most important single factor that has been contributing to an increase in Australian content over the recent period has been Australian tariff policy. He also notes that more than 91 percent of the imports came from foreign affiliates, as compared with a figure of about 70 percent reported in the Department of Trade and Commerce survey for 1965.[16]

Exports by American direct investment firms in manufacturing in the United Kingdom compare very favourably with those in both Canada and Australia. In 1965 such U.K. firms exported 25 percent of their total sales, compared with a national average for manufacturing of about 14 percent. This difference is partly explained by the larger size of American subsidiaries and their greater representation in some major exporting industries. But even when American firms and other U.K. firms compete side by side, the American firms have a better export sales performance. This superior export performance is partly related to such factors as favourable marketing arrangements with parent firms abroad and specialization relative to the parent, given unit production costs which are usually below those of the parent. It also may reflect decisions by the British authorities to admit some foreign firms with high export potentials.

American subsidiaries in the United Kingdom achieved also a higher than average growth of manufacturing exports from 1957 to 1965. Nearly one-third of the growth of all manufacturing exports in these years was accounted for by American firms. In 1965 such firms accounted for 9.6 percent of manufacturing output, but 17.5 percent of the United Kingdom's manufacturing exports.[17]

---

[15] Brash, *op. cit.*, pp. 220-40.

[16] *Ibid.*, pp. 203-12.

[17] Dunning, *The Role of American Investment in the British Economy*, pp. 120 138, and 148. For his earlier study of exports, see Dunning, *American Investment in British Manufacturing Industry*, pp. 56, 291-95.

5

The Research and Development
Performance
of Foreign-Owned Firms

In many earlier discussions of foreign investment, the emphasis was on the transfer of capital to the recipient company. In recent years, more and more emphasis has been placed on the importance of the transfer of technical information and skills of a wide variety — in management, research and development, production, and so on. It has become increasingly clear that these transfers of techniques are at the very heart of the process of direct investment. At the same time, there has been much concern that the ease of getting such techniques from the parent company may militate against the development of similar skills in the subsidiary, to the detriment of the development of national skills.

Industrial Research and Development Expenditures in Canada

The role of research and development expenditures in Canada and in some other countries is shown in Table 10. As a percentage of gross national product, research and development expenditure in Canada was only half that in the United Kingdom and only one-third that in the United States. Many factors would account for this, including differences in mix of industry and in size of firm. A larger proportion of the research and development expenditures in Canada are concentrated in government laboratories than is the case in any of the other countries shown. As a percentage of gross national product, however, this expenditure in government laboratories in Canada works out to about the same as in the United States, the United Kingdom, the Netherlands, and France

41

TABLE 10

COMPARATIVE EXPENDITURE ON RESEARCH AND DEVELOPMENT, BY COUNTRY, 1963-64

Country	Year	As a % of GNP	Done by (percentages)			Paid by (percentages)		
			Business	Higher Education	Government[a]	Business	Higher Education[b]	Government
United States	1963-64	3.4	67	12	21	32	4	64
United Kingdom	1964-65	2.3	67	7	26	42	4	54
Netherlands	1964	1.9	56	20	24	54	6	40
France	1963	1.6	51	11	38	33	3	64
Sweden	1964	1.5	67	18	15	49	2	48
Japan	1963	1.4	65	19	16	65	7	28
Germany	1964	1.4	66	20	14	57	2	41
Canada	1963	1.1	41	14	45	34	11	55
Belgium	1963	1.0	69	20	11	71	5	24

[a]Includes private non-profit of 11 percentage points for Germany, 21 for the Netherlands, and 4 or less for others.

[b]Includes private non-profit and funds from abroad. Data for Canada also include indirect support of research by government through normal university grants.

Source: Organisation for Economic Co-operation and Development, *A Study of Resources Devoted to R and D in OECD Member Countries in 1963-64*, pp. 14 and 57. Figures include capital but exclude depreciation.

and to more than in the other countries. Again relative to gross national product, government financial support of research in Canada in 1962-63 was less than one-third that in the United States and less than half that in the United Kingdom.

A notable difference between Canada and other countries is in industrial research done by business firms; industrial research, at 41 percent of all research and development expenditures in Canada, was well below that of any other country shown in Table 10. In terms of research *paid* for, industry's proportion of the total in Canada ranked lowest with those of the United States and France. As a percentage of gross national product, industrial research expenditure in Canada in 1962-63 was lower than for any of the other countries shown. The Science Council of Canada notes that a large part, though not all, of this difference, by comparison with the United States and the United Kingdom in particular, reflects government support of research in industry in the latter countries through defense and other contracts.[1]

The extent of access to the research and development and know-how of the parent company by the subsidiary cannot be doubted. In Safarian's study, fully 187 of 215 firms reporting on this point indicated that the research and development and know-how of the parent firm were fully available to them. In 18 other cases as well, there was some degree of access. Access extended not only to the parent's research and development as normally understood, but also to a great variety of skills represented in production, marketing, administration, and investment in plant and equipment. A related point is the fact, shown by the same study for about the same number of companies, that about 80 percent of them had access to either the patents or the copyrights — and, in most of these cases, to both the patents and the copyrights — of the parent companies. In the majority of cases, moreover, the research and development and know-how of the parent company were available to the subsidiary without charge or for a nominal payment, although, in a substantial minority of cases, full cost or something approximating it was paid. The reason why full payment was usually absent would appear to be partly that charges are sometimes levied in other ways — for example, through pricing on products imported from the parent — and partly that the parent firm in any case receives the profits of the subsidiary or, if dividends are not paid out, the value of the Canadian subsidiary's assets is increased. The undercharging for business services of this kind may also reflect an attempt to minimize the over-all tax paid by the international firm — that is, to concentrate more of its profits in Canada in periods when the effective rate of corporation income tax is lower than in the United States. In any case, it is quite clear that any study of the actual amounts paid for business services of various kinds, such as research and development, know-how, management fees, and so on, will understate both the actual value of these services and the real nature of the costs involved.[2]

Thus Table 11, based on information supplied under the Corporations and Labour Unions Returns Act, cannot be taken as a measure of either the value or

---

[1] Science Council of Canada, *First Annual Report, 1966-1967*, p. 5.
[2] Safarian, *op. cit.*, pp. 189-96.

TABLE 11

PAYMENTS BY CANADIAN COMPANIES TO NON-RESIDENTS FOR VARIOUS
BUSINESS SERVICES, BY DEGREE OF NON-RESIDENT OWNERSHIP, 1964
(millions of Canadian dollars)

Type of Payment	Ownership by Non-Residents	
	Under 50%	50% or over
Royalties	16.6	52.8
Franchises	7.4	22.6
Advertising	5.6	17.5
Research	4.2	29.8
Insurance premiums	3.0	10.3
Management fees, salaries, annuities	6.9	64.8
Professional services, other	12.7	38.3
Total	56.4	236.1

Source: CALURA, *Report for 1964*, p. 21.

the total payments for such business services. It represents a selection of the
various kinds of business services paid abroad, as reported under the Act, which
are most likely to be related to direct investment as such. It should be added
that there is no official breakdown showing payments to parent companies or
affiliated companies abroad, but rather only payments to all non-residents.
Nevertheless, some of the payments, such as royalties, management fees, and for
research, are particularly likely to be payments to the parent companies.
(Insurance premiums and possibly some aspects of professional services may not
be as fully related.) It will be noted that Canadian companies whose voting stock
was owned 50 percent or more abroad made payments of $236.1 million to
non-residents for the selected business services in 1964, while companies owned
less than 50 percent abroad made payments of only $56.4 million for these
services.

Research Performance of Subsidiaries in Canada

The question which is relevant in the present context concerns the
performance of the subsidiary firms and, specifically, the view that, since the
parent companies are already undertaking extensive research, the subsidiaries are
necessarily doing less than they might, with serious consequences for the
development of research in Canada. The economic literature on this point
cannot be used to settle this issue. In many industries there are good reasons for
centralizing research and development, while in others there are equally good
reasons for decentralizing it — or at least for specialization between the various
parts of the affiliated companies. The question essentially revolves around the
economies of decentralization of research and development, which in turn are related to economies of scale for such research activity, the need for adapting to
local conditions, and, in some industries, the need to do research and development as part of the production process. Nor can one overlook the fact that ac-

cess to the research of the parent often provides advantages to the subsidiary firm — for example, in taking advantage of previous research and in avoiding some types of mistakes.

What are the facts about industrial research and development in Canada? The view that the subsidiary companies do little research must be severely qualified on the basis of the only available comprehensive statistics on industrial research in Canada. The Dominion Bureau of Statistics conducted a survey in 1955 which has been repeated every second year since then. It will be noted from Table 12 that fully 58 percent of the current intra-mural research and develop-

TABLE 12

CURRENT INTRA-MURAL RESEARCH AND DEVELOPMENT EXPENDITURES
IN CANADA, BY INDUSTRY, 1966
(millions of Canadian dollars)

	Expenditures	Percentage Distribution
Mines, gas and oil wells	10.7	4.3
Manufacturing:		
Food and beverages	6.1	2.5
Rubber	3.1	1.3
Textiles	3.2	1.3
Wood	0.3	0.1
Furniture and fixtures	0.1	–
Paper and allied products	16.2	6.5
Primary metals (ferrous)	4.0	1.6
Primary metals (non-ferrous)	10.3	4.2
Metal-fabricating	3.2	1.3
Machinery	8.9	3.6
Aircraft and parts	50.8	20.5
Other transportation equipment	1.8	0.7
Electrical products	60.5	24.4
Non-metallic mineral products	2.1	0.8
Petroleum products	15.7	6.3
Drugs and medicines	8.3	3.3
Other chemical products	24.9	10.0
Scientific and professional instruments	7.9	3.2
Other manufacturing [a]	4.1	1.7
Transportation and other utilities	3.7	1.5
Other non-manufacturing [b]	2.1	0.8
Total	248.0	100.0

[a] Includes tobacco products, leather products, clothing and knitting mills, and miscellaneous manufacturing industries.

[b] Includes the construction industry, scientific and engineering services, and trade associations.

Source: Dominion Bureau of Statistics, *Industrial Research and Development Expenditures in Canada*, 1965, p. 20. Intra-mural expenditures are those for work performed within the reporting company; extra-mural, those for the R & D performed by other firms and organizations for the reporting company. Extra-mural expenditures in 1966 were $37.9 million, of which $27.1 million were spent abroad.

ment expenditures in Canada in 1966 are concentrated in three industries: aircraft and parts, electrical products, and drugs and other chemical products.[3] At the end of 1963 foreign control of the non-automobile transportation industry was 78 percent; of electrical apparatus, 77 percent; and of chemicals, 78 percent, A number of other industrial groups which, in absolute terms, spend major amounts on research and development also have a substantial degree of foreign control of their capital, including such industries as mining, petroleum products, and paper and allied products. It should be added that the aircraft and parts

TABLE 13

CURRENT INTRA-MURAL RESEARCH AND DEVELOPMENT EXPENDITURES IN CANADA AS A PERCENTAGE OF SALES, BY INDUSTRY, 1965[a]

Industry	% of Sales	Industry	% of Sales
Aircraft and parts	16.7	Primary metals: ferrous	0.5
Scientific and professional		non-ferrous	0.9
instruments	6.7	Paper	0.6
Other non-manufacturing [b]	4.9	Petroleum products	0.6
Electrical products	4.8	Other manufacturing [b]	0.6
Drugs and medicines	4.5	Metal-fabricating	0.5
Other chemicals and products	1.7	Non-metallic mineral products	0.5
Rubber	1.2	Furniture and fixtures	0.3
Mines	1.0	Food and beverages	0.2
Textiles	1.0	Wood	0.2
Machinery	0.9	Other transportation equipment	0.1
		Transportation and other utilities	0.1

Average, all industries 1.1

[a]These are the sales (excluding the sales of goods purchased for re-sale) only of those firms reporting payments for R & D performed in Canada.
[b]See footnotes to Table 12 for coverage.

Note: Strictly comparable data on foreign ownership are not available in all cases. At the end of 1963, foreign control of capital in the electrical apparatus industry was 77%; chemicals, 78%; rubber, 97%; mining, 51-62%, depending on the sector; automobiles and parts, 97%, and other transportation equipment, 78%; textiles, 20%; pulp and paper, 47%; petroleum and natural gas, 74%; beverages, 17%; railways, 2%, and other utilities, 4%. Residents appear also to own the majority of the capital in the furniture and fixtures and the wood industries, and probably in metal-fabricating and non-metallic mineral products, all of which do below-average research as a percent of sales. See Dominion Bureau of Statistics, *The Canadian Balance of International Payments*, 1961 and 1962, pp. 83 and 133, and 1963-65, Table 19.

Source: Dominion Bureau of Statistics, *Industrial Research and Development Expenditures in Canada*, 1965, p. 42.

industry and the electrical-products industry received quite large sums through contracts and grants from the federal government in aid of their research. It is also true, however, that the latter industry spent more of its own funds on research than any other industry shown, and the former was the fourth largest

---

[3]For definitions, see Table 12.

spender, in absolute terms.[4] It will be noted from Table 13 that dollars spent on Canadian research and development in 1965, as a percentage of sales, rank electrical products, drugs and other chemical products, and aircraft and parts above the average for industry generally.

What this demonstrates, of course, is simply that foreign-owned firms tend to be in research-oriented industries, and no more than this. The data do suggest, however, that one should be careful about simple statements relating the relatively small part of Canadian national product devoted to research to the presence of foreign-owned firms as such. Somewhat more sophisticated data on such comparisons will be presented shortly.

In view of the frequent references made to the research performed or not performed by foreign-owned firms in Canada, it is surprising to have to record that the only official study of industrial research and development expenditures in Canada does not break these down according to country of ownership of the firm. This is a defect in these statistics that should be remedied if we are to begin to understand fully the role of foreign-owned subsidiaries in domestic research.

The only private study of the research performance of foreign-owned firms in Canada is reproduced in Table 14. These data refer to the year 1959. Since that year there has been a considerable upsurge in industrial research spending, due partly to federal government aid. The definition used to measure research and development was patterned closely on that used by the Dominion Bureau of Statistics in its studies of industrial research and development. It states:

> Activities directed to pure or basic research (i.e., to programs not primarily committed to specific product or process application) and also to conceiving and developing new products, new processes and major changes in products and processes and bringing them up to the stage of production. Such activities as market and sales research, process and quality control and geological and geophysical exploration, should be excluded. If in doubt, please use your normal definition and briefly specify its nature.

It will be noted that 109 of the firms did some research and development, as defined, within the Canadian company; fully 129 did no research and development within the Canadian company; while 42 firms failed to answer this question. A group of 73 firms reported purchases from affiliates outside Canada, including 43 which were doing research and development within the Canadian company. (Actual access to the parent company research goes well beyond *payments* for such research, as noted earlier.) Finally, 16 firms purchased research from other firms or organizations. In all, 141 firms had some sort of a research effort defined as research within the firm, payments for purchases from affiliates abroad, or payments to other firms or organizations; 93 had no research effort as just defined; and in 46 cases no reply was available. There appeared to be no significant difference in the research performed within the Canadian company when a distinction was made between subsidiaries owned in

---

[4] Dominion Bureau of Statistics, *Industrial Research and Development Expenditures in Canada*, 1965, p. 23.

TABLE 14

COST OF RESEARCH AND DEVELOPMENT AS A PERCENTAGE OF TOTAL ANNUAL SALES, 1959
(number of firms)

Research and Development as % of Sales	(1) Done Within the Canadian Company	(2) Purchased from Affiliates Outside Canada	(3) Purchased from Other Firms or Organizations	(4) Totals Indicating Some or No Form(s) of (1), (2), and/or (3)
Zero percent	129	153	191	93
Up to 0.5	23	21	7	19
0.6 - 1.0	22	9	1	21
1.1 - 2.0	26	9	–	33
2.1 - 5.0	16	10	–	26
Over 5.0	3	1	1	6
% unspecified [a]	19	23	7	36
Subtotal	109	73	16	141
No reply to question	42	54	73	46
Total	280	280	280	280

[a]These firms indicated they were doing research and development as defined, but did not give the percentage to sales. Many of them indicated the research effort was small, probably under one percent of sales.

Note: There is duplication among the first three columns in the sense that any single firm could theoretically answer all three questions. The fourth column reflects the total research effort included in (up to three of) the previous columns.

Source: A. E. Safarian, *Foreign Ownership of Canadian Industry*, p. 176.

the United States and those owned by overseas interests. The larger firms were more likely to be doing research; but among those firms doing research there was no marked relationship between research as a percentage of sales and the size of the firm. In other words, if there are economies of scale with respect to research, they do not show up very clearly in this series.[5] There was a strong positive relationship between research and development as a percentage of sales and the size of the Canadian firm *relative* to the affiliate. Particularly worth noting is that, where the products of the subsidiary were generally identical to those of its affiliate, only 25 percent of the firms did research, but where the products were differentiated in various degrees, fully 68 percent of the firms did some research.[6]

Comparison of Subsidiaries in Canada with Parents and with Resident-Owned Firms

These data clearly suggest that there is a significant research program in a considerable number of subsidiary companies in Canada. How do these programs compare with those of the foreign affiliates? In 79 of the firms performing research in Canada, sufficient detail was given to permit an assessment of this question. In at least one-third of the parent firms there were programs not primarily committed to specific product or process applications ("basic research"), a proportion well beyond that in the Canadian subsidiaries, as indicated below. The parents' programs were also oriented more to conceiving and developing new products than were those of the subsidiaries. Finally, it was possible to get comparisons of relative spending by the two sets of firms in the case of 96 subsidiaries. In 69 of these (72 percent), spending on research and development as a percentage of sales was considerably less than in their foreign parent firms. In 22 subsidiaries (23 percent), it was roughly the same, and in 5 others (5 percent), such spending was considerably more as a percentage of sales. In brief, while the programs of the subsidiaries were extensive, they were not as highly developed on a relative basis as were those of the parent companies, nor were they oriented as much to basic research.[7]

This does not answer the question whether, in general, access to research from abroad militates against the development of research spending in Canada. Safarian made three separate and distinct tests of this particular question.

---

[5] Safarian made a more extensive test of the relationship between industrial research as a percentage of sales and the size of the firm by combining the non-resident-owned firms in his study with the resident-owned firms. He arrived at 136 observations, which were considered within four size groups and within 16 industry groups. These showed a slight tendency for research and development as a percentage of sales to fall within industry groups as the size of the firm rose between the four size categories used. This test, which is more conclusive than that mentioned in the text, also raises questions about the extent of economies of scale with respect to research and development. See Safarian, *op. cit.*, p. 179.

[6] *Ibid.*, pp. 177-82.

[7] *Ibid.*, pp. 185-86.

In the first place, 76 firms rated access to the knowledge of the affiliate as indispensable or highly important, while other firms rated such access all the way from important to (as indicated by some replies) of little or no importance or not applicable to the firm. If one examines the research programs in Canada of the 76 firms, a rather interesting point comes to light. Of those firms in this group which did no research and development in Canada, 28 percent indicated that access to the parent's research and development was indispensable or highly important. Of those firms which were spending up to one percent of sales on research and development in Canada, 28 percent again indicated that access to the parent's research was indispensable or highly important. For the firms in this group spending more than one percent of sales on research and development in Canada, however, 36 percent rated access to the parent's knowledge this highly. While one may not wish to give much significance to differences of this magnitude, they do suggest that where access to the parent's knowledge is very important, this need not militate against the establishment of research and development facilities in Canada.[8]

TABLE 15

COST OF RESEARCH AND DEVELOPMENT DONE WITHIN
THE CANADIAN COMPANY IN 1959, RESIDENT-OWNED AND
NON-RESIDENT-OWNED COMPANIES WITH ASSETS OF $1 MILLION OR MORE
(percentages except bottom row)

Research and Development as Percentage of Sales	Asset Size in $ Millions						All Firms	
	1 - 4.9		5 - 24.9		25 and over			
	R	NR	R	NR	R	NR	R	NR
0	54	58	43	36	31	31	46	46
Up to 0.5	10	4	33	8	44	34	25	12
0.6-1.0	8	8	7	17	6	3	7	9
1.1-2.0	3	13	7	17	–	16	4	14
2.1-5.0	15	10	3	3	6	9	9	8
Over 5.0	5	–	3	3	–	3	4	1
% unspecified	5	7	3	17	13	3	6	9
Total	100	100	100	100	100	100	100	100
No reply and not available as % of over-all total	5	13	14	16	20	9	11	13
Number of firms above	41	82	35	43	20	35	96	160

Note: R means owned by residents, NR by non-residents. Totals may not add due to rounding.

Source: A. E. Safarian, *Foreign Ownership of Canadian Industry*, p. 281.

---

[8] *Ibid.*, p. 198.

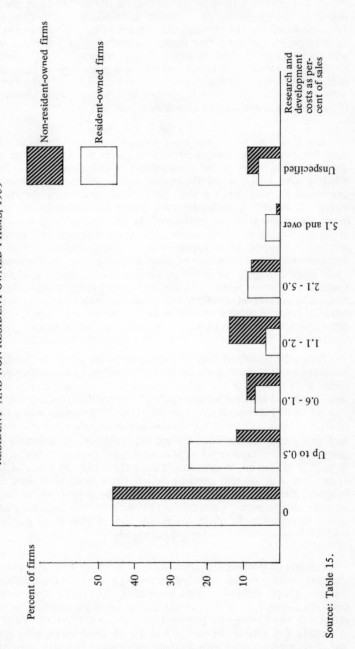

CHART 3

RESEARCH AND DEVELOPMENT COSTS AS PERCENTAGE OF SALES,
RESIDENT- AND NON-RESIDENT-OWNED FIRMS, 1959

Non-resident-owned firms

Resident-owned firms

Research and development costs as per-cent of sales

Percent of firms

Source: Table 15.

A second test was made by classifying the 280 firms in the study by the degree of foreign ownership — that is, according to whether the parent owned 100 percent of the voting stock, 75 percent or more of the voting stock, or less than 75 percent of the voting stock. Research spending as a percentage of sales was then related to these three ownership categories. By this test, there is no consistent relationship between research as a percentage of sales and the actual degree to which the foreign parent holds the stock of the Canadian company. In other words, the differences in research performance when classified by degree of foreign ownership were not significant statistically.

The third test was to compare research and development as a percentage of sales for 160 foreign-owned firms with assets of $1 million or more and 96 resident-owned firms in the same industries with assets of $1 million or more. Whether one looks at all expenditures for research and development as a percentage of sales (both within the firm and payments outside the firm), or simply at research and development within the company, the results are the same. About the same proportions of the two sets of firms were doing research in 1959. For those firms which were doing research and development, the non-resident-owned firms appeared to be doing somewhat more research and development as a percentage of sales than were the resident-owned firms. In other words, roughly the same proportions of the two sets of firms engage in research and development, but the non-resident-owned firms do more of it in relation to sales. If one confines one's attention only to manufacturing firms, the safest conclusion would appear to be that there is no statistically significant difference between the research effort of the two sets of firms.

It should be added that the research programs of the foreign-owned and resident-owned firms appear to be fairly similar. In about one-quarter of each group with such programs, the improvement of products and/or processes was a significant part of their program; about two-thirds in each group reported that conceiving and developing new products and/or processes was a significant part of their program, along with improvement of existing products and processes. In each group only 10 percent reported that programs not primarily committed to specific product or process applications were important within the Canadian firm. It is of interest to note that, among the firms with assets of $25 million or more, not one of the resident-owned firms considered that uncommitted programs formed a significant part of its research program. In fact, in the two sets of firms together, eight of the twelve firms with such programs had assets under $25 million. In other words, the size of firm is no guarantee that the research programs will be more sophisticated.

It might be thought that the access to the parent's research and development program would give the non-resident-owned companies important advantages in competing with resident-owned companies. No doubt there is much to this point. However, it should be noted that some of the resident-owned firms have offset this disadvantage by getting access to the research of non-affiliated firms in Canada and abroad. In fact, 32 of the 96 firms which were resident-owned had made arrangements with unaffiliated firms or industry associations outside

Canada for access to their knowledge or to their property rights or to both.[9]

On the basis of present evidence, we must question the view that the non-resident-owned firms in Canada do not perform a significant amount of research, or do not perform research as frequently as their resident-owned counterparts, or do not perform as sophisticated research as their resident-owned counterparts. It is clear that they do not do as much research or as sophisticated research as their parent companies abroad in most cases. One might also take the position that, given the access to the research of their parent companies, better performance might be expected of the non-resident-owned firms than of their resident-owned counterparts in this question of research. Finally, we wish to emphasize that the environment of public policy regarding research support is an important determinant of industrial research activity. A large part of the difficulty until recent years has been that government aids to research and development have been rather limited in comparison to what has been available elsewhere, with the consequence that the industrial research performance of firms in Canada has been less than it might be. This point is given more emphasis if we consider the experience of the United Kingdom, where there has been a more substantial research orientation than is the case in Canada.

Subsidiary Performance in the United Kingdom and Australia

In his book on American direct investment in British manufacturing, Dunning distinguishes between fundamental research (which seeks to advance knowledge), applied research (the exploitation of new knowledge with a specific object in mind), and development research (the stages which elapse between the inception of an idea and its full commercialization on the factory floor). In his sample of firms, 25 percent noted that they maintained no separate research and development department. These firms were most likely to be those which produced products identical to those of their American affiliates, were small and established recently, and whose policies were closely supervised by the parent. In 56 percent of the subsidiaries there was some applied and development research, while the firms relied on their American associates to provide them with fundamental research in particular. In this group there was considerable adaptation of American products to British needs. In 19 percent of the subsidiaries some basic research was undertaken on their own. In such cases, however, there was close liaison with the parent-company research facilities.

Dunning underlines the importance of research potentially available from the parent firms by noting that, in real terms, the parent companies of the 100 most important American-financed firms manufacturing in the United Kingdom spent more on research and development each year than all of British industry combined. Also, 43 percent of American-affiliated firms in his sample made no direct payments for the research and development knowledge which they received. He notes that, in addition to the research and development, the manufacturing experience of the parent company and its affiliates and their management methods are also available to the subsidiary. In some cases such

[9] *Ibid*, pp. 280-86 and 295.

manufacturing and management experience may far outweigh the benefits derived from access to research and development as such.[10] He goes on to warn that overreliance on Americans for research and development may not be healthy in all cases if it restrains the undertaking of independent research and the demand for the development of scientists and technicians.

It is evident that a somewhat larger proportion of the firms in Dunning's sample were engaged in research and development, and that more of them were doing fundamental research, than is the case with the group of foreign-owned firms studied by Safarian in Canada. The contrast is greater if we bear in mind that the Dunning study precedes by several years the study of the firms in Canada, since in both countries the incidence of research and development in industry has been increasing rapidly. To some extent the superior performance of the American firm in British manufacturing industry reflects the comparatively stronger support given by the government to industrial research in that country at that time, but it may well also reflect the fact, noted earlier, that American-owned firms in British manufacturing are highly oriented to manufactured exports. Cause and effect become intermingled in issues of this kind. It is also necessary to add the qualification that differing definitions of research and development in the two studies complicate comparisons of this type, both with the United Kingdom and with Australia.

Brash found that 57 percent of the American-owned firms he studied in Australia did not do research in 1962, as compared with 45 percent of the foreign-owned firms studied by Safarian for Canada for the year 1959. This difference may not be meaningful, given the differences in the definition of research, in industry mix, in size of company, and so on. Brash notes that only a very small amount of basic research is conducted in Australia by the American-affiliated firms, although their product development is significant. At the same time, his data suggest that the longer a company is established in Australia, the greater is the likelihood that it will undertake research. He goes on to note that it is possible that American-affiliated firms devote a higher portion of their resources to research than do other firms in the Australian economy, although the comparisons are not as precise as he would like. The 99 American-affiliated firms he studied employed on average more than twice as many research staff in their factories as did Australian industry as a whole in 1961-62. He notes that the importance of the motor vehicle industry affects the over-all picture and that, in only six of the ten industries where comparison was possible, did American-affiliated firms employ relatively more research staff than the Australian industry in question. The six industries, however, are among the most important of the ten.[11]

A Broader Question

In this section we have examined the research performance of foreign-owned firms in Canada, partly in absolute terms and partly by comparison with other firms. We have not tried to come to grips with the basic issue of the proper

---

[10] Dunning, *American Investment in British Manufacturing Industry*, pp. 164-77.
[11] Brash, *op. cit.*, pp. 147-54.

strategy to be followed by governments in regard to the developing of technology. It may be pointed out, however, that the advantage which the foreign-owned firm frequently enjoys over its Canadian competitors is concentrated especially in the area of technology — research and development, production experience, management methods — rather than simply in its accessibility to capital or in its market contacts. Thus, if any effort is to be made to increase the degree of Canadian participation in Canadian industry, close attention must be paid to the means of strengthening the technological and management base of resident-owned industries. At the same time, it is well to point out that foreign-owned firms in Canada have access to many of the most outstanding industrial laboratories in the world. On the basis of the research performance of the non-resident-owned firm in Canada and of Canadian industry generally, as discussed above, it is difficult to believe that Canadians have learned to take maximum advantage of this access. It is true that the government of Canada and some provincial governments have made strong efforts in recent years to increase the research consciousness of industry and to offer specific aids and tax concessions towards this end. Much remains to be done in making the maximum domestic use of the foreign research available to Canada, on the one hand, while effectively developing research initiatives by residents, on the other. The success of such initiatives is related to larger issues regarding the development of a more efficient industrial structure, a topic we will consider later.

Intercompany Pricing

No general study has yet been made in Canada of the implications of intercompany pricing of exports, imports, and business services of various kinds. It is known that many of the intercompany prices are quite different from arm's-length or market prices, the usual intent probably being to minimize the over-all tax paid by the international firm. The fear has been expressed that such pricing may not be in the Canadian interest in that there may be overpricing of components, materials, and business services of various kinds bought from the parent, and underpricing of exports to the parent. No study on trade is available, but Safarian's findings for research and development, know-how, and patents indicate the contrary for the late fifties, in that most of the direct investment companies were charged nothing directly for these or were charged only a nominal value. This finding is not conclusive, since the charges may have been made in other ways, such as through the pricing of products to the subsidiary.

The clue to such practices may best be found in the attempt by the international company to minimize the over-all tax paid in the various national jurisdictions. Until the last few years, the effective rate of corporation income tax in Canada was probably less than in the United States. It made sense for the parent company to throw more of its profit to the Canadian subsidiary, through underpricing of imports of goods and services into Canada and overpricing of exports. Insofar as profits were retained in Canada, the higher rate of effective tax in the United States could be avoided. In the past few years this situation has changed, partly because the two effective rates of corporate income tax have become about the same and partly because the American corporate guidelines regulations encourage parents to charge subsidiaries something closer to an arm's-length price in order to increase receipts by the United States. In these circumstances it is important that the Canadian taxation authorities ascertain that there is not overpricing on imports of goods and services and underpricing on exports by the Canadian subsidiaries, for if there is, Canada will not be maximizing her tax revenue from the operations of subsidiaries. It appears that in recent years the taxation authorities have been checking this more closely, but it is not clear whether this check is comprehensive enough yet.

It may be noted that, in terms of wholly owned direct investment companies, the Canadian interest is basically that mentioned — maximizing tax revenue. In most other respects, it does not matter if arm's-length pricing is not followed in trade between affiliates, except possibly if questions of dumping arise. Overpricing of imports, for instance, reduces profits and dividend payments abroad; and so on for other examples of over- or underpricing. Other interests become involved if minority stockholders exist in the subsidiary. Something like arm's-length pricing must then be used in order to prevent subsidies accruing to the minority stockholder on the one hand or to the major owner on the other.

6

The Returns to the Owners

The financial aspects of direct investment in Canada are a matter of considerable importance. This section will examine returns on direct investment received by the owners, whether these returns are retained in Canada or paid abroad. In addition, we shall take up a related question that has aroused much criticism in Canada, namely, the practice of most of the firms involved of reserving their voting stock completely for the parent. Finally, since most of the other international transactions of foreign-owned firms have already been considered up to this point, an attempt will be made to draw up an over-all statement concerning the direct effects of these firms on the Canadian balance of payments.

Ownership Structure of Canadian Subsidiaries

In terms of the ownership of voting stock, the situation is quite clear. The great majority of the parents prefer to own all the voting stock of their subsidiaries. Returns under the Corporations and Labour Unions Returns Act indicate that in 1963 there were, in the manufacturing and mining industries in Canada, 1,961 corporations each having the characteristic that at least half its stock was held outside Canada. In 72.1 percent of these firms, 95 percent or more of the voting stock was held outside Canada. In most of the latter firms the parent company held 100 percent of the voting stock, except for directors' qualifying shares. In 12.6 percent of the firms, 75 to 94.9 percent of the stock was held by non-residents. In 15.2 percent of these firms, 50 to 74.9 percent of the stock was held by non-residents. The corresponding proportions for the particular service and financial industries covered in the Corporations and Labour Unions Returns Act were 70 percent, 11.7 percent, and 18.3 percent.[1]

---

[1] CALURA, *Report for 1963*, p. 18.

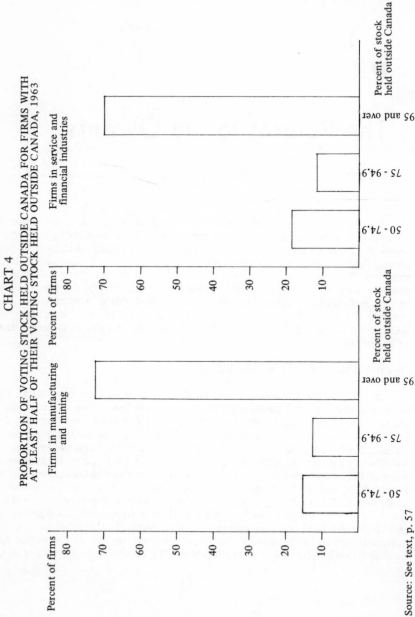

CHART 4

PROPORTION OF VOTING STOCK HELD OUTSIDE CANADA FOR FIRMS WITH
AT LEAST HALF OF THEIR VOTING STOCK HELD OUTSIDE CANADA, 1963

Source: See text, p. 57

Another way of examining such data is to consider the location of the ownership of the over-all investment in foreign-controlled enterprises in Canada.

TABLE 16

STRUCTURE OF OWNERSHIP OF INVESTMENTS IN ALL
FOREIGN-CONTROLLED ENTERPRISES IN CANADA, END OF 1965
(percentages)

Ownership of investments by residents of:	Country of Control			
	U.S.	U.K.	Other Foreign	Total
1. Country where parent is located:				
Unincorporated branches	10	6	3	8
Canadian corporations	70	50	63	67
	80	56	66	75
2. Canada:				
Debt	8	21	20	12
Equity	10	15	7	10
	18	36	27	22
3. Other countries	2	8	7	3
Total	100	100	100	100

Source: Supplied by courtesy of the Dominion Bureau of Statistics.

Table 16 shows that, at the end of 1965, 75 percent of the investments were owned by residents of the country where the parent was located, 22 percent by residents of Canada (less than half of which were in equity and over half in debt), and 3 percent by residents of other countries. Still other data suggest that, if one considers solely the equity investment of all foreign-controlled enterprises in Canada at the end of 1960, only 15 percent of it was owned by Canadians. The comparable figure for enterprises controlled in the United States was 14 percent, and for enterprises controlled in other countries, 21 percent. It appears that the larger firms are more likely to issue equity. In the case of firms which had an investment in Canada of $25 million or more and which were controlled abroad, 19 percent of their equity was held by Canadians, as compared with only 9 percent in the case of enterprises whose assets were less than $25 million.[2]

---

[2] Dominion Bureau of Statistics, *The Canadian Balance of International Payments*, 1961 and 1962, p. 89.

The data collected by Safarian showed that 71 percent of the firms do not issue any stock. Firms with assets of $25 million or more have a much smaller percentage of wholly owned companies among them than do the smaller firms, although more than half the firms with assets of $25 million and more in his study were wholly owned by the parent. In five industries, 40 percent or more of the firms had issued stock; these industries were petroleum, primary mining, paper products, primary metals, and chemicals. Some of the largest foreign-owned firms are producing primary products or are engaged in primary manufacturing processes. In these types of industries some financing by the public or by independent Canadian firms may be more customary than in secondary manufacturing.

The strong preference of the parent companies for full ownership of the voting stock of the subsidiaries can be noted in another way. Safarian secured data for 242 firms on the changes or absence of changes in the parent companies' degree of ownership. Potentially, each of the 242 firms could, over the period since the relationship with the parent company was first established, have decreased the parent company's ownership of voting stock. In fact, only 22 did so. In seven of these 22 cases the decreases were smaller than five percentage points; and in nine of them the minority stock issue was closely held by another firm or by a small group of individuals. All but 70 of the 242 firms began with 100 percent initial ownership by the parent. In 32 of the 70 firms the parent had increased its ownership of the Canadian firm since the link with the latter had been established; in 9 cases the increase was to the 100 percent level. In all but 5 of the 32 cases where increases took place, the increases exceeded five percentage points. In most of the cases in which a minority stock issue now exists, the reason appears to be that the firm was begun as a joint venture with another Canadian firm or that the subsidiary reflects only a partial take-over of the Canadian firm by the parent company at the time the relationship was first established.[3]

It is of interest to note one further study of this question. On March 31, 1966, the Minister of Trade and Commerce wrote to many subsidiary companies, setting forth some guiding principles of good corporate behaviour. The tenth guiding principle was "to have the objective of a financial structure which provides opportunity for equity participation in the Canadian enterprise by the Canadian public." An analysis of the 885 replies (covering many more separate firms than this number) is very revealing of company attitudes to this question. This principle and a related one on the publication of financial data were the only ones — of the twelve guiding principles — with which more of the replies disagreed than agreed and with which more of the firms indicated they did not conform than indicated they did conform. The specific numbers are that 116 replies disagreed with this guiding principle on various grounds, while 75 agreed; and fully 497 of the respondents indicated that they did not conform, while 58 indicated that they did conform. The reason so many do not conform is that they are classed as private companies in Canada. Under Canadian law a private company is one with less than fifty shareholders, the parent company being counted as one shareholder. As a consequence, the many subsidiary companies

---

[3] Safarian, *op. cit.*, pp. 222-28.

in Canada that are wholly owned by the parent and do not offer shares in their operations to the general public are classed as private companies. It should be added that private companies are not required to publish financial detail on their operations. Thus, in regard to the guiding principle "periodically to publish information on the financial position and operations of the company," the replies followed closely those in regard to the guiding principle on equity participation. In 104 of the replies concerning disclosure, there was disagreement with the guiding principle; in 27 replies, agreement; meanwhile, 469 of the respondents indicated they did not conform, and only 49 indicated that they did conform.

Why do so many foreign-owned firms persist in refusing to issue shares in spite of the fact that strong urgings to issue shares have been expressed by Canadian governments and that, in 1963, various tax incentives were introduced to encourage such issues?

1.   One reason, already cited, is the fact that issuance of shares would mean that financial information would have to be reported to the public. Presumably, private firms are reluctant to do this, partly because they do not see the point to it when there are no public shareholders and partly because they enjoy a competitive advantage over their publicly owned competitors, who have to publish financial information. This advantage would be eliminated and other useful purposes would be served if all but the smallest Canadian firms were required to disclose financial data, although Canadian firms would then be at a disadvantage with respect to any competitors in foreign countries who did not issue similar data.

2.   A second reason is that the owners are unwilling to share the earnings of the firms that they have developed or acquired and have turned into successful operations.

3.   A third reason for this reluctance is the fact that companies differ a good deal in the size and complexity of their operations, the degree of integration with the parent, and their ability to market their shares successfully.

4.   A fourth reason lies in a number of technical problems involved in the issue of shares, such as the difficulty and timing of share issuance, given the stage of growth of the subsidiary and its needs for capital; its earnings record, which may be rather erratic in the early phases of the subsidiary; the desire to plow back earnings to aid rapid growth, rather than to establish a dividend policy; and the need to price intercompany transactions in terms of market prices in order to avoid subsidization to either the minority shareholders or to the owners of the parent.

5.   Finally, the most important reason for the reluctance to issue shares may well be that the issuance of shares diminishes the flexibility with which the subsidiary and the parent can deal with each other. Decisions about the location of plant and production, financing of activity, and the exchange of information are all much easier to make when dealing with wholly owned subsidiaries than

when dealing with subsidiaries in which there are minority shareholders whose interests must also be taken into account. The parent company is not as free, for example, to put capital into a rapidly expanding subsidiary, since the minority shareholders must be asked to supply some of the capital and since the minority shareholders may not take kindly to the decision to retain earnings for expansion. The decision to locate export production according to the most efficient source may not be made as readily in a situation where some of the profits must be shared with minority shareholders. Moreover, complete ownership may be preferred, in part, because such intercompany arrangements with a partly owned subsidiary are more likely to be subject to American anti-trust law.[4]

Needless to say, such considerations as these, which highlight the problems for the subsidiaries, must be set in a context of the advantages or disadvantages that Canadians in general receive as a result of efforts to encourage the issuance of shares. The advantages might include such developments as a more active capital market in Canada, a reduction in dividend payments abroad, and a reduced capital outflow into foreign shares, depending on how the minority shares were financed. The major cost may be not the significant tax incentives apparently required to secure such issues, but rather the diversion from other uses of large amounts of scarce Canadian equity capital in order to purchase non-controlling shares in existing productive enterprises.

Ownership Structure of Other Subsidiaries

Data are available to indicate that the preference by American parent companies for full ownership of their foreign subsidiaries pertains to those in other countries abroad as well as to those in Canada. The only detailed study of this in recent years was the census of U.S. direct investments for the year 1957. That study indicated that nearly three-quarters of U.S. direct investment abroad was in enterprises in which the American share of equity was at least 95 percent, including foreign branches of U.S. companies. About one-fifth of the total was in enterprises where the percentage of U.S. ownership ranged from 50-95 percent, and about 5 percent was in enterprises where the American participant had a minority interest but where the aggregate U.S. equity was at least 25 percent. The study goes on to note that over half the minority holdings were in Canada. In part this may reflect the fact that there are several large direct investment companies in Canada, particularly in mining, which have no parent company abroad but have substantial Canadian minority holdings of their stock. Enterprises established since 1946 show a moderate shift towards lower proportions of U.S. equity participation as compared with enterprises established prior to that time, particularly in the case of Canada and Europe. The American and foreign ownership of the equity and of the related surplus and reserves in American direct investment companies abroad is shown in Table 17. The non-American ownership of the equity and surplus is greater for Canada than for any other area shown, with the exception of the relatively small

---

[4] *Ibid.*, pp. 230-34.

investment in Africa. At the same time, in no area is the non-American ownership much in excess of one-quarter of the total.

TABLE 17

U.S. AND FOREIGN OWNERSHIP OF EQUITY AND
SURPLUS OF AMERICAN ENTERPRISES, BY AREA, 1957
(millions of U.S. dollars)

	Stock, Surplus, and Surplus Reserves	
	U.S. Ownership	Foreign Ownership
Canada	5,297	1,684
LatinAmerica	2,764	541
Europe	3,371	681
United Kingdom	(1,751)	(400)
France	(406)	(64)
Germany	(464)	(45)
Africa	312	110
Asia	733	115
Oceania	428	85
Australia	(395)	(79)
International [a]	617	1
Total	13,522	3,218

[a]International refers to certain shipping operations of petroleum and shipping companies in particular. Latin America includes other western hemisphere.

Note: Data exclude finance and insurance.

Source: U.S. Department of Commerce, *U.S. Business Investments in Foreign Countries,* p. 108.

The data collected by Dunning suggest there is a considerable decline in the extent to which American manufacturing affiliates in the United Kingdom remain 100-percent-owned as the age of the firm increases. For example, of the 31 American-financed firms operating in 1953 which were established before 1914, only 16 were still completely American-owned in 1953. Yet 12 of the balance of 15 began as 100 percent American-financed subsidiaries. The percentage of wholly owned subsidiaries rises as one comes closer to 1953 as the date of establishment. Dunning suggests that the subsidiaries which are 100 percent American-owned tend to be those which supply products identical or nearly identical to those of their parents, use similar manufacturing methods, rely heavily on American research, and supply export markets previously served from the United States. On the other hand, those that have reduced the amount of American financial participation tend to be those whose products or processes must be adapted to the differing conditions in the United Kingdom.[5]

---

[5] Dunning, *American Investment in British Manufacturing Industry,* pp. 97-98.

The study by Brash of American-affiliated firms manufacturing in Australia in 1962 indicated that 125 out of the 208 firms were either branches or wholly owned subsidiaries of American companies, 5 had between 75 and 99 percent of their voting shares owned in the United States, for 50 firms the percentage was between 50 and 74, and for the remaining 28 firms the percentage was between 25 and 49. (The definition of direct investment used in both the American data and Brash's Australian study includes firms in which the American firm owns 25 percent or more of the voting stock.) It appears that there has been some change over time in favour of sharing ownership, according to the data by Brash. However, it may be noted that, although 83 of the 208 firms were jointly owned, the weighted average ownership for the entire group was more than 88 percent American in 1962.[6]

Brash goes into some detail concerning the reasons American firms prefer to retain the shares in their Australian subsidiaries. Many of the reasons he gives are parallel to those noted above in regard to the Canadian case. He notes that participation by Australians may become a means whereby the foreign firm gains control over increased resources while the minority shareholders achieve little control over important aspects of company policy. His extended discussion of this subject concludes that local participation in equity is unlikely to have many advantages from Australia's point of view, while the immediate costs of such participation would require significant diversion of capital from other projects. He suggests that if foreign capital inflow has disadvantages, there are better ways of controlling these than through minority participation.[7]

Rate of Return to Parent on Operations of Canadian Subsidiaries

A brief look at the sources of funds of U.S. direct investment companies in Canada is useful for providing perspective to the ensuing discussion. Table 18 shows that during the past decade between 60 percent and 80 percent of the funds used by these firms have come from sources internal to the subsidiary, specifically in the form of net income and depreciation. Funds from the United States fell off as a proportion of the total after 1958, partly because of monetary conditions in the two countries, but also because petroleum and mining, which tend to rely more heavily on funds from the United States, were more important relative to manufacturing in the earlier part of the period. There has been a significant recovery, however, in the proportion of funds coming from the United States. The remaining category, which consists mainly of funds from Canada outside the subsidiaries, has recently been higher than at any time during the past decade. Unfortunately, data on sources of funds, in the form used here, are not available beyond 1965.

Our concern here is with the net income portion of these funds — that is, with the return to the parent company. The Canadian interest, barring cyclical

---

[6] Brash, *op. cit.*, pp. 59-64.
[7] *Ibid.*, pp. 67-78.

fluctuation, presumably is that these returns to the parents, after Canadian taxes, be as small as is consistent with the retention of the investments in Canada and their efficient operation. It is not possible to state any particular figure which would generally reflect this desirable level of return, but it is possible to make certain comparisons with resident-owned companies and with direct investment companies in other parts of the world. The importance of this point will be clear if one considers that the gains from foreign investment can appear in a variety of forms. They can appear, for example, in the quality and price of the products made available to the host country. They can appear in a superior performance in certain other respects on the part of the subsidiaries. They might appear also, however, in superior profits to the parent company and eventually in either a higher dividend return to the parent or a greater increase in its assets in Canada.

TABLE 18

SOURCES OF FUNDS, ALL U.S. DIRECT
INVESTMENT COMPANIES IN CANADA, 1957-65
(percentages)

	1957	1958	1959	1960	1961	1962	1963	1964	1965
Funds from the United States	26	25	20	21	13	10	8	5	19
Funds from Canada outside the subsidiary a	13	14	11	-1	12	15	14	18	20
Net income	35	32	39	45	41	43	45	48	37
Depreciation	26	30	30	35	34	32	33	29	25
Total	100	100	100	100	100	100	100	100	100

a Also includes funds from other countries and from small miscellaneous sources.

Source: Calculated from data in U.S. Department of Commerce, *Survey of Current Business,* various issues. Data refer to all U.S. direct investment firms in Canadian manufacturing, mining, and petroleum industries.

The only source of data on profits of direct investment companies in Canada is CALURA, as summarized in Table 19. For the first time detailed industrial data concerning the returns on direct investment, including breakdowns by degree of foreign ownership, have become available. If one concentrates on those commodity-producing sectors in which non-resident ownership is particularly large — namely, manufacturing, mining, and petroleum — it would appear that the returns to direct investment are not very different from the returns to the resident-owned sectors of the same industries. Thus, in 1962-64, profits before tax in these industries were as follows:

	1962	1963	1964
As a percentage of equity			
Resident-owned firms	14.8	16.1	17.6
Non-resident-owned firms	14.0	14.4	16.6
As a percentage of sales			
Resident-owned firms	8.8	9.3	9.9
Non-resident-owned firms	9.8	9.9	11.0

TABLE 19

PROFITS BEFORE TAX AS A PERCENTAGE OF EQUITY,
BY DEGREE OF FOREIGN OWNERSHIP AND BY INDUSTRY, 1962-64
(percentages)

Industry	1962		1963		1964	
	R	NR	R	NR	R	NR
Mining, refining, mineral fuels:	9					
Metal mining	9.5	10.1	12.6	13.3	14.5	19.4
Other mining	6.4	13.4	4.1	15.8	8.4	16.7
Primary metal industries	19.1	16.2	23.5	15.8	22.4	24.2
Mineral fuels	4.4	6.1	5.0	8.1	7.4	7.4
Petroleum and coal products	7.4	8.7	12.6	4.3	20.0	8.3
Primary manufacturing:						
Food	14.4	17.1	15.6	17.3	16.4	21.4
Beverages	31.3	24.9	31.3	33.1	34.6	22.0
Tobacco	23.1	18.7	24.9	17.2	22.9	16.9
Leather	10.5	6.3	10.3	7.1	14.3	13.3
Wood	9.1	16.2	15.8	19.8	15.0	21.1
Paper	15.7	16.3	16.1	14.5	17.8	17.7
Non-metallic mineral products	17.4	15.1	16.0	15.3	17.5	20.3
Secondary manufacturing:						
Rubber	15.2	9.5	31.8	13.6	23.5	11.0
Textiles, knitting, clothing	12.8	23.2	14.1	22.4	15.8	20.6
Furniture	9.5	13.3	10.3	13.2	16.1	12.9
Printing and publishing	18.9	19.1	19.9	18.0	22.5	21.2
Metal fabricating	11.1	15.9	12.6	19.1	15.6	19.4
Machinery	9.3	21.6	9.9	23.9	16.3	25.8
Transportation equipment	11.0	25.1	15.8	30.5	15.5	23.1
Electrical products	15.0	10.3	18.1	13.3	18.8	17.7
Chemicals	11.1	18.3	16.3	20.1	16.8	21.0
Miscellaneous	14.8	23.5	13.7	19.2	15.0	22.4
All industries	14.8	14.0	16.1	14.4	17.6	16.6

Note: R means resident ownership of firms is over 50 percent; NR means non-resident ownership is 50 percent or more.

Source: Derived from CALURA, *Report for 1964*, pp. 56-76.

There are obvious problems in comparing such figures, given the fact that there are substantial intercorporate financial items involved, different procedures for valuing equity, and different degrees of processing of sales by industry. It must be emphasized that such comparisons merely compare all foreign-owned and all resident-owned firms (excluding the smallest), although the product mix of the two sets of firms differs considerably. For example, the resident-owned portion of equity in the petroleum and coal products industry is quite tiny compared with the non-resident-owned sector of that industry. It should also be added that the profits of the non-resident-owned firms are probably overstated, since less than full charges were paid by many of these firms to the parent for the services supplied to them.

If one considers 22 major commodity-producing industries, profits as a percentage of equity were higher for the non-resident-owned groups of firms than for the resident-owned — in 15 industries in 1962, in 13 in 1963, and in 12 in 1964. This comparison favours the non-resident-owned firms more strongly if profits as a percentage of sales are used, but this measure seems less reliable where different degrees of integration of production are likely. It must be admitted that the spread between the average profits of the two sets of firms is fairly small in several industries and often could easily be accounted for by some of the problems of measurement noted above. It would appear, on the whole, that profits of non-resident-owned firms are about the same as, or only moderately higher than, those of resident-owned firms. The one qualification one should make to this is if one considers only the secondary manufacturing industries classified separately in Table 19. In the ten such industries shown, profits as a percentage of equity were higher for non-resident-owned firms in 8 cases in 1962, 7 in 1963, and 6 in 1964. The results are more striking for profits as a percent of sales, where in each year 9 industries (all but rubber) show higher profits for the non-resident-owned firms. A more precise test would involve examining the profitability of resident-owned and non-resident-owned firms when the two are roughly comparable in size of firm, product mix, and other variables.

Another set of data, given in Table 20, shows the returns on American direct investment by areas abroad. These figures are after foreign tax, while the data from CALURA mentioned above are before Canadian tax. It will be noted that in 1967 the return on American direct investment in Canada by this measure was less than in any other major area in the case of manufacturing, and was less than any major area except Europe for all industries taken together. The same source for 1965 shows Canada yielding the lowest return among the major areas in the case of all industries, and the lowest after Latin America in the case of manufacturing. Data for individual countries show more variation than this, of course. Such comparisons are also considerably affected by the mix of industry involved in the various regions. Nevertheless, they suggest that the returns on American direct investment are not high in Canada by comparison with such returns elsewhere.

It is important to add that the returns on direct investment are more than the profits of the firms involved. The parent firm also receives various kinds of royalties, management fees, and other returns for technical services rendered. Such payments abroad to parent companies and other firms were shown in Table 11. It is a little difficult to know whether these should be related to the equity of the firm as such, since presumably there is some cost to the parent in transmitting the services for which these returns are received. If the firms have a minority share issue, it is likely that the royalties and other payments can be related more accurately to the equity base, since both will probably have been adjusted to avoid subsidization to the minority shareholders or to the parent. Where most of the companies are wholly owned, the valuations placed both on equity and on intercompany services, as well as on the pricing of intercompany trade on commodity account, may all be quite arbitrary for purposes of calculating rates of return. It was noted earlier that the payments for various kinds of business services probably understate considerably their value. Finally, in the context of the international firm, the returns may be looked at much more broadly than the direct monetary returns discussed up to this point. For example, the parent may regard its foreign subsidiary as a stable source of supply or a guaranteed outlet for the parent's manufactured parts, so that the subsidiary's value may well reflect more than the direct monetary return.

TABLE 20

RATES OF RETURN[a] ON AMERICAN DIRECT INVESTMENT ABROAD,
ALL INDUSTRIES AND MANUFACTURING, 1967, BY AREA
(percentages)

	All Industries	Manufacturing
Canada	7.8	8.0
Latin America	12.2	8.2
Europe	7.0	10.7
United Kingdom	6.7	9.1
France	3.4	5.9
Germany	7.2	12.5
Africa	20.2	13.8
Asia	34.5	18.7
Oceania	8.3	12.5
Australia	7.9	11.9
All areas	11.0	9.3

[a]Returns are the sum of the U.S. share in net earnings of subsidiaries and branch profits, a sum applied to the book value of investments at the end of 1966 in order to get the rates of return shown above.

Source: Derived from *Survey of Current Business,* October, 1968, pp. 24-25.

Return on American Subsidiaries in Australia and the United Kingdom

Brash notes that a large group of Australian-owned manufacturing companies surveyed by the Reserve Bank of Australia earned only 6.9 percent on shareholders' funds in 1962. Of the 79 American-owned companies studied in this connection by Brash, 43 earned more than 6.9 percent of the value of their American investment. One large and very successful American company in Australia considerably affects the results of his study. This company, which accounted for 40 percent of total U.S. earnings on direct investment in Australian manufacturing, raised the average return on the value of American investment from 7.7 percent to 11.4 percent. Brash goes on to note that for 72 companies the return on the American investment becomes 9.2 percent instead of 7.9 percent — that is, about 16 percent higher — if one includes interest and fees (such as royalties, fees for technical services) in the return earned by the American parent. This measure is based on the assumption that no extra cost accrues to the American company in supplying the technical information to the Australian affiliate. Brash concludes that, on the average, American direct investment has been more profitable than Australian or British investment in manufacturing, but that the higher American return is particularly affected by the very successful performance of the largest American firm.[8]

Dunning found the average rate of return on the capital of American-owned firms in the United Kingdom was substantially in excess of that for the leading U.K. public companies in manufacturing. The former was about 90 percent higher than the latter in the fifties, but this excess fell sharply to about 40 percent in the first half of the sixties. For the period 1950-66 the leading U.K. public companies earned 8.7 percent on capital, as against 14.9 percent for American-owned firms. His research suggests this difference cannot be ascribed in the main to differences in the industrial distribution of the two sets of firms, to accounting differences, or to arbitrary charges between parent and subsidiary. He concludes that the difference largely reflects the superior efficiency of the American-owned firms, along with the access they have to the expertise of the parent.[9]

Payment of Earnings Abroad

One of the important differences between bond financing and equity financing is in the nature of the return involved. In the case of financing by bonds, a fixed interest return is payable, and the bonds come up for redemption, usually at a specific point of time. Thus the liability involved is known, and the opportunity arises at a particular point of time to repatriate the bond at a fixed price. This can cause a problem if the income available to finance the interest and repatriation should decline and if refinancing becomes difficult for other reasons. For example, during the 1930s interest payments by Canadians to non-residents were rigid, and in some cases they increased because they were payable in several currencies at the lender's option. This turned out to be a difficult situation for many private and public bodies to handle, since their receipts had declined, as had the country's international receipts. The return paid out on direct investment, on the other hand, is flexible and depends on the

---

[8]*Ibid.*, pp. 250-51, 262.
[9]Dunning, *The Role of American Investment in the British Economy*, pp. 130-36.

extent to which the subsidiary earns income and on the decision as to the proportion of income to be paid out. Moreover, while the subsidiaries can be repurchased by acceptable bids, and a number are each year, there is no particular point of time and no fixed price at which such repatriation comes up for consideration. Indeed, if the firm has been successful, its price will have increased accordingly. In many cases, moreover, the subsidiary is so closely integrated in its technology or marketing with the parent company that its acquisition by other interests is difficult to conceive.

For present purposes we need note only two points. The first is that the return on direct investment is unknown and continues as long as the subsidiary prospers. The payout on direct investment, in turn, depends on the profits of the subsidiary and on the decision as to the extent to which these profits are to be paid out. Apart from being an indeterminate return, it is quite clear that in direct investment companies the actual payments are going to be irregular, since they will reflect the needs of both the domestic subsidiary and the parent concerning expansion and other variables. There could be complete retention of earnings for substantial periods of time if rapid growth is involved for the subsidiary, combined with payments in excess of current earnings when decisions to pay are made. The second point to note is that, so long as the firm is foreign-owned and is successful in its operations, the increase in its assets is, in effect, an increase in foreign investment. In other words, unlike bond investment, where specific decisions are made to import or not to import capital at particular points of time, the growth of the foreign-owned firm leads to an automatic increase in foreign-owned investment in the country, provided that the firm is successful and that some earnings are retained within the subsidiary. It will be obvious from this that there are quite different balance of payments implications for bond and direct investment. The balance of payments effect through bond financing is known and fixed, whereas that through direct investment is indeterminate, involves an increasing contingent liability, and may be erratic.[10]

The burden of the foreign interest and dividend debt accumulated by Canada in the last decade or so, insofar as it is reflected in current payments abroad, does not appear to have been high relative to earlier experience. Thus interest and dividends paid abroad as a percentage of gross national product were 2.9 percent in the late twenties and 6.4 percent in the thirties. In the period 1957-67 inclusive, they amounted to 1.9 percent. These payments abroad can be related also to the earnings available from the export of goods and services, since these earnings are available to finance these and other payments. As a percentage of export earnings, interest and dividends paid abroad fell from 16 percent in the late twenties and 25 percent in the thirties to 9 percent in the period 1957-67 inclusive. Unfortunately, comparable data for other earnings by non-resident owners from their investments in Canada are not available. Table 11 indicates that companies whose stock was owned 50 percent or more abroad in 1964 paid

---

[10] See E. T. Penrose, "Foreign Investment and the Growth of the Firm," *Economic Journal*, June, 1956, pp. 220-35, for a discussion of these characteristics of direct investment.

out to non-residents $236 million for royalties, franchises, advertising, research, insurance premiums, management fees, salaries, and other professional services. It is not possible to say, however, what portion of these payments went to the parent companies. Another measure is that reported in the Department of Trade and Commerce study of foreign-owned subsidiaries in Canada. This showed that the 266 larger direct investment companies in Canada paid abroad $251 million in 1965 for such items as royalties, management fees, advertising, and research, but excluding interest and dividends. By comparison, total payments abroad of interest and dividends, by *both* resident-owned and non-resident-owned firms, were $1,048 million in 1965, a figure which had risen to $1,310 million in 1968.

The measures given above for the burden of interest and dividends paid abroad pertain to all payments both by resident-owned firms and by non-resident-owned firms, as well as by all levels of government. Some of the comments above about the nature and size of direct investment payments abroad can be demonstrated more directly if we concentrate on payments abroad by non-resident-owned companies only, as shown in Table 21.[11] It will be noted that the percentage of after-tax income which was paid abroad was as low as 40 percent in 1953 and as high as 64 percent in 1950. In the mid-fifties the proportion was very low, between 40 and 43 percent, reflecting the need to retain earnings in Canada for expansion in a period of relatively rapid growth. In the late fifties and early sixties the percentage distributed abroad rose to as high as 57 percent in 1961. It will also be noted that during the late fifties undistributed earnings fell, but the amounts sent abroad continued generally to rise. In brief, the relationship between earnings and income paid need not be a close one over short periods of time. Very substantial amounts were retained in Canada by these firms during the postwar period — amounts which went to expand direct investment in Canada. Indeed, the undistributed profits of direct investment firms from 1946 to 1961 were equivalent to about 40 percent of the over-all increase in direct investment during the period.

Some of the tendencies noted above can be discussed in more detail if we examine the 228 firms which gave information on dividend payments abroad in the study by Safarian. Over half the firms in that study paid no dividends at all in the 1950s. Sixty-nine of them indicated they paid up to 49 percent of their net earnings as dividends during that decade, and only 36 that they paid more than this amount. Of the 228 firms only 11 paid out 75 percent or more of their earnings during the decade. Of course, many of the firms established in the fifties did not pay dividends during the first few years of their operations. Even when classified by age of the firm, however, the data show a considerable amount of flexibility in regard to the payment of dividends. For example, significant numbers of firms which had been in Canada more than ten years paid no dividends, or paid dividends of less than one-quarter of their earnings, in the decade of the fifties. The data also indicate that a higher percentage of earnings was paid as dividends during that decade by firms which had a minority stock issue (particularly if the minority stock issue was widely held) than by firms in

---

[11] These figures do not include the payments for business services referred to in the previous paragraph.

which the parent owned all the stock. It should be emphasized that a number of the wholly owned firms, especially among the larger ones, declare an annual dividend which is a fixed percentage of net earnings, but in most cases there is a more flexible approach to dividend payments in the direct investment firm. This is not to suggest that the parent does not expect a paid return from its direct investment operations. Insofar as dividends are concerned, however, returns are considered on a longer-term basis than is true in publicly owned companies, where a regular dividend payment is much more common.[12]

TABLE 21

TOTAL RETURNS ACCRUING TO ALL FOREIGN DIRECT INVESTMENTS IN CANADA, 1946-64
(millions of Canadian dollars)

Year	Remitted Income	Allowance for Withholding Tax	Undistributed Earnings	Total Earnings	Percentage of Earnings Distributed Abroad
1946	147	12	120	279	53
1947	183	15	125	323	57
1948	174	14	160	348	50
1949	233	19	155	407	57
1950	309	25	150	484	64
1951	272	23	190	485	56
1952	239	22	295	556	43
1953	217	22	305	544	40
1954	230	22	280	532	43
1955	274	26	335	635	43
1956	310	26	400	736	42
1957	340	24	425	789	43
1958	339	23	235	597	57
1959	365	24	350	739	49
1960	318	28	280	626	51
1961	396	57	240	693	57
1962	398	52	305	755	53
1963	424	52	410	886	48
1964	562	58	455	1,075	52

Source: Dominion Bureau of Statistics, *The Canadian Balance of International Payments: A Compendium of Statistics from 1946 to 1965*, pp. 174-75.

The difference in Canada between direct investment companies and resident-owned firms can be highlighted by comparing such firms with assets over $1 million, as is done in Table 22. Fully 39 percent of the non-resident-owned firms paid no dividends at all in the fifties, compared with 13 percent of the resident-owned firms. In addition, 22 percent of the non-resident-owned firms paid half or more of their net earnings as dividends, compared with 37 percent of the resident-owned firms. Among the firms with assets of $25 million or more, about a third of the non-resident-owned group paid no dividends in the

---

[12] Safarian, *op. cit.*, pp. 247-53.

decade of the fifties, in contrast with the fact that all the resident-owned firms paid dividends during that decade. As noted before, many of the new firms did not pay dividends at first. But even if one concentrates on only those firms over ten years old, the differences in dividend payments as a percentage of net earnings still exist.[13] These conclusions are consistent with over-all data for all Canadian companies. These data show that for the period 1952-60 all the direct investment companies taken together paid 44 percent of their net earnings. Since all companies in Canada, including direct investment companies, paid about half of their earnings, the resident-owned firms alone must have paid well in excess of half.[14]

TABLE 22

PERCENTAGE OF NET EARNINGS PAID AS DIVIDENDS, 1950-59,
RESIDENT-OWNED AND NON-RESIDENT-OWNED CANADIAN COMPANIES
WITH ASSETS OF $1 MILLION OR MORE

Percentage of Net Earnings Paid	All Firms		Assets of $25 Million or More		All Firms over 10 Years Old	
	R	NR	R	NR	R	NR
0	13	39	–	31	10	30
1 - 24	14	15	18	16	14	16
25 - 49	36	25	35	28	38	28
50 - 74	32	18	35	25	30	21
75 - 100	5	4	12	–	7	5
Total percentage	100	100	100	100	100	100
Number of firms above	76	131	17	32	69	86
No reply and not applicable	20	29	3	3	18	20
Total firms	96	160	20	35	87	106

Note: R refers to resident-owned, NR to non-resident-owned. Seven of the former and six of the latter, established before 1950, gave data for a period shorter than 1950-59.

Source: A. E. Safarian, *Foreign Ownership of Canadian Industry,* p. 293.

The greater flexibility in dividend payments by foreign-controlled firms reflects the fact that public shareholders require in most cases some sort of a regular dividend policy, whereas a single parent company may not. The effect, apart from the fact that foreign ownership is increased because a larger proportion of dividends is retained, is to give the subsidiary much greater flexibility in financing investment from retained earnings. In other words, the subsidiary is in a strong position to undertake projects without being as much

---

[13] *Ibid.*, pp. 289-90.
[14] Dominion Bureau of Statistics, *Canadian Balance of International Payments,* 1960, p. 22.

concerned about sources of financing by comparison with its resident-owned counterpart. When combined with the access the subsidiary has to financing from the parent, this may mean that the subsidiary is in a much stronger position than its resident-owned counterpart to undertake investments that have a longer time horizon in terms of payoff.

American direct investment in Canada pays out a significantly smaller proportion of its earnings than is true of American direct investment elsewhere. In 1967 American direct investment in Canada paid out 51 percent of its earnings, against 74 percent in all countries, according to estimates by the U.S. Department of Commerce. These percentages are considerably affected by the fact that American direct investment in mining and petroleum pays out a much larger proportion of its earnings in other countries than of its earnings in Canada. Thus the proportion of earnings distributed in petroleum for all countries in which there was such American direct investment was 92 percent in 1967, compared with only 55 percent for Canada. The corresponding percentages in the case of mining were 82 and 66. If we restrict ourselves to manufacturing industries alone, the proportion of earnings paid out by American direct investment in all countries was nevertheless higher than for Canada, namely, 59 percent against 44 percent. Data for 1965 too show significantly smaller proportions paid out in the case of Canada, except in manufacturing where the proportions were close.[15]

Brash's figures for 66 American-affiliated companies in Australia largely confirm the statements made above in the Canadian case. He notes that the average ratio of dividend to after-tax profit is smaller for the wholly American subsidiaries than for jointly owned ventures. Moreover, American-owned enterprises are generally more conservative in their dividend policy than are British-owned Australian enterprises.[16]

Effects on Balance of Payments

The question of the over-all balance of payments implications of direct investment is too large and complex to be dealt with adequately here. It should be clear, however, that one cannot treat the question of dividend and other payments abroad in isolation. Direct investment has had an effect in raising Canadian income and therefore the capacity to meet the growing income payments abroad due to direct investment. From the standpoint of the balance of payments, the relevant question is how these payments abroad relate to the

---

[15] *Survey of Current Business*, October, 1968, and September, 1966.

[16] It may be noted here that Brash suggests that a conservative dividend policy may be due only in part to a desire to build up the local investment. It may be due in part also to the desire to avoid Australian withholding tax on dividends paid to the United States. He suggests that this is tied in with the preference for 100 percent ownership, for it is easier in these cases to manipulate intercompany accounts in order to minimize the impact of the withholding tax. The specific point noted by Brash is that significant amounts of loans on an intercompany basis, and the interest paid on these, may take the place of dividends and of shareholders' equity when it is to the advantage of the parent company to use this type of financing. Brash, *op. cit.*, pp. 68, 90-91.

export-earning and import-replacing achievements of foreign-owned firms in Canada. In addition, there are substantial continuing capital inflows which add to Canada's foreign exchange reserves, at least in the first instance. Indeed, it can be argued that, while such payments abroad may fluctuate significantly in the short run, in the longer run the capacity to make such payments abroad — dividends in particular — is going to be related to the earnings of the foreign-owned companies. In turn these earnings are significantly related to exports and import replacement. In other words, one would expect that the payments abroad and the net foreign exchange contributions of these firms would tend to move together over longer periods.

A study by the Department of Trade and Commerce makes it possible to give an approximate estimate of the direct over-all effects that foreign investment by parent companies abroad has on the Canadian balance of payments. The word "direct" should be emphasized, since foreign investment has a number of indirect but important consequences for Canadian incomes and foreign trade. Moreover, foreign investment itself modifies the use of existing resources and hence their potential effects on trade. Unfortunately, no study is available for Canada of the over-all adjustments in the balance of payments caused by direct investment. The direct effects are summarized for the larger firms in Table 23, which shows the international transactions of 266 larger firms from which data were collected under the Canadian guidelines procedures. It will be recalled that

TABLE 23

SUMMARY OF INTERNATIONAL TRANSACTIONS OF
266 LARGER DIRECT INVESTMENT COMPANIES IN CANADA, 1965
(millions of Canadian dollars)

	With the United States	With Other Foreign Countries	Total
Current transactions:			
Exports	1,732.5	1,013.4	2,745.9
Imports	-2,077.6	- 605.3	-2,682.9
Merchandise balance	- 345.1	408.1	63.0
Other current receipts	20.7	34.0	54.7
Dividend payments [a]	- 312.0	- 40.0	- 352.0
Other current payments	- 223.6	- 27.8	- 251.4
Non-merchandise balance	- 514.9	- 33.8	- 548.7
Current-account balance	- 860.0	374.3	- 485.7
Selected capital transactions	459.1	22.3	481.4
Over-all balance	- 400.9	396.6	- 4.3

[a]Includes 10 - 15 percent paid to the Canadian federal government as withholding taxes.

Source: Department of Trade and Commerce, *Foreign-Owned Subsidiaries in Canada*, p. 11.

these figures overstate merchandise imports, since they include in some cases payments to the Canadian government for tariff duties and for internal transportation charges. They also overstate dividend payments abroad in that something like 10 to 15 percent of the total reflects withholding taxes paid to the Canadian federal government. On the receipts side, since the figures for exports relate to only the final exporters, some Canadian grain shipments have been included as exports through foreign-owned distributors. If these factors could be adjusted they would tend to have offsetting effects on the balance of payments, but their sizes are not known.

It will be noted that in 1965 the 266 larger firms had a deficit on merchandise trade with the United States, but a surplus with overseas countries, to give an over-all surplus of $63 million. Other current transactions, particularly dividend payments and payments for business services, resulted in a deficit of $549 million. Thus there was a deficit on current-account balance — that is to say, on merchandise and non-merchandise account — of $486 million. The data also measure certain capital inflows from abroad from both affiliates and other sources, including loans, advances, other credits, and investment in equity. These amounted to $481 million in 1965, so that, taking the current transactions and the measured capital transactions together, the direct effects on the balance of international payments work out almost to zero in 1965. It will be noted that this direct effect is made up of an over-all current and capital deficit of $401 million with the United States and a surplus of $397 million with overseas countries.

Another way to look at these figures is to consider trade with the parent company and other foreign affiliates abroad as distinct from that with non-affiliated groups. It then becomes clear that the deficit on current account is attributable to transactions with the parents and other affiliates abroad. In 1965 these recorded a deficit on trade alone of $535 million, and on trade plus non-merchandise items a deficit of fully $982 million. There was a surplus on trade and non-merchandise transactions with non-affiliated groups abroad which offset $496 million of the deficits with affiliated entities.

Similar patterns appear in 1964 on current account, where the 266 larger subsidiaries show a surplus of $333 million on their total foreign trade, and a deficit of $493 million on non-merchandise transactions, resulting in a current-account deficit of $160 million. While the data are not comparable to Canada's over-all balance of payments figures conceptually, it is interesting to note that in 1965 Canada had a current-account deficit of $1,136 million and in 1964, a current-account deficit of $433 million. The over-all merchandise trade surplus, as measured in Canada's balance of payments data, was $101 million in 1965 and $700 million in 1964. The contribution of these companies to the selected capital transactions noted earlier is not available for the year 1964.

To turn to the industry detail for the merchandise trade and non-merchandise transactions of these 266 companies, it will be noted that most of the industry groupings show a deficit in their international current transactions in 1965. Table 24 may be compared with Table 8, which showed merchandise trade alone for the various industrial groups covered by the 266 firms represented in Table 24. Only in mining and primary metals, pulp and paper, and wholesale trade do surpluses appear on merchandise plus non-merchandise account. The largest single deficit on current account was concentrated in the transportation-equipment industry, a deficit that has been sharply reduced in the past few years. Only one other industry showed a deficit on current account in excess of $200 million. The deficits are heavily concentrated in particular in transactions with affiliates abroad, and particularly in merchandise trade transactions with the affiliates, as indicated in Table 24.

TABLE 24

CURRENT INTERNATIONAL BALANCE OF 266 LARGER DIRECT
INVESTMENT COMPANIES IN CANADA, BY INDUSTRY AND AFFILIATION, 1965
(millions of Canadian dollars)

Industry	All Transactions		With Affiliates Only	
	Merchandise	All Current Transactions	Merchandise	All Current Transactions
Mining and primary metals	289.4	239.4	188.9	155.1
Gas and oil	- 61.7	-173.2	-137.4	-219.1
Machinery and metal fabricating	-175.0	-222.4	-131.5	-176.8
Transportation equipment	-609.5	-711.1	-457.8	-543.6
Electrical products industry	- 63.2	- 92.1	- 62.0	- 87.2
Chemical products industry	- 81.8	-125.1	- 55.7	- 95.4
Food and beverage industry	- 51.5	- 85.3	- 23.3	- 54.9
Pulp and paper industry	699.9	622.3	286.0	232.7
Other manufacturing industry	- 97.8	-135.0	- 81.3	-115.7
Wholesale trade industries	263.3	253.2	- 51.4	- 61.2
Other non-manufacturing	- 49.2	- 56.4	- 9.0	- 15.6
Total	63.0	-485.6	-534.5	-981.7

Source: Department of Trade and Commerce, *Foreign-Owned Subsidiaries in Canada,* Appendices IV and VI.

7

The Efficiency of Foreign-Owned Firms in Canada

One of the key questions about foreign-owned firms in Canada is the question of how efficiently they operate and supply Canadian needs. An efficient firm is one that operates with the lowest attainable average cost of production. This implies that the firm has the ability to meet competition from domestic and foreign sources in supplying customers. It also implies that it can earn a sufficient return to capital and to labour, under competitive conditions, to maintain its operations over the longer run without long-term protection or subsidy. This question of the efficiency of foreign-owned firms is clearly related to the question of the benefits that Canadians derive from foreign investment.

It must be admitted that here, more than elsewhere, one feels the lack of adequate governmental and private studies of the relative performance of foreign-owned firms. One must be satisfied with data which are statistically inadequate, such as profit figures, or are conceptually merely approximations of what is desired, as is the case with data on output per employee and on cost per unit of output. This chapter will outline briefly what is known in these respects about the characteristics of the foreign-owned firm and will relate this to the larger question of the structure of Canadian industry.

Limitations of Relevant Data

In order to study the efficiency of the foreign-owned sector, one must pass from data outlining the financial facts of ownership to data of the sort published in the Canadian census of manufactures and in other such industrial reports. Unfortunately, the integration of the extensive data on ownership of enterprises — data which have been collected for some years in Canada — and of the long-standing series on production has not yet proceeded as far as one would like for the present purpose. Neither the study of foreign-owned subsidiaries in Canada, prepared jointly by the Department of Trade and Commerce and the Dominion Bureau of Statistics, nor the material prepared under CALURA gives data which can be used to assess the efficiency of the foreign-owned firm. The single important exception is the profit data supplied by the reports under CALURA.

The single study that is by a government agency and that illuminates the efficiency question is the Dominion Bureau of Statistics' survey of the manufacturing operations in Canada of larger foreign-owned enterprises. This was first conducted for the year 1946 and was followed up for 1953, and the most recent follow-up was for 1961. The earlier two of these studies cover only subsidiaries controlled in the United States with assets of $1 million or more in Canada in terms of book value, while the 1961 study includes, for the same assets range, Canadian subsidiaries controlled in other foreign countries as well as those controlled in the United States. Apparently it was necessary to exclude from these studies the many thousands of smaller firms (with assets under $1 million) because of the difficulty and the time which inclusion would require. It is true that the larger foreign-owned firms (with assets of $1 million or more) account for a very large proportion of over-all foreign investment in Canada. In 1961 the firms covered by the study accounted for almost 95 percent of all foreign-controlled investment in Canadian manufacturing industries. Unfortunately, the exclusion of the smaller companies considerably complicates the use of these data for our major purpose — that of comparing foreign-owned firms with resident-owned firms. Any such comparison is complicated to an unknown extent: on one side of the comparison, only the foreign-owned firms with assets of $1 million or more are included; the other side of the comparison includes not only resident-owned firms with assets of under, as well as over, $1 million, but *also* foreign-owned firms with assets of under this figure. It is very likely that the resident-owned firms with assets of under $1 million would account for much more than the 5 percent indicated above as the share that foreign-owned firms with assets of under $1 million represent in the total for foreign-owned firms in manufacturing. The one size group for which comparisons between resident-owned and non-resident-owned firms can be made, in terms of the present set of questions, consists of those firms with assets of over $25 million. The differences noted below between resident-owned and non-resident-owned firms are therefore exaggerated, except in the case of firms with assets of over $25 million.[1]

---

[1] The production data are based on the concept of the establishment which is the smallest independent operating unit for which the required input and output data can be obtained and which is therefore classifiable to an industry. A number of establishments may form a corporation, while an aggregation of corporations under common ownership and financial control is referred to as an enterprise. The book-value data on foreign investment are generally derived from consolidated balance sheets of enterprises in Canada.

The Record for Canada

The key data from the 1961 Canadian survey are presented in Table 25. Turning first to the group of foreign-owned manufacturing establishments with assets of $1 million or more, we see that the 1,464 such firms represented 4.5 percent of the total of 32,415 manufacturing establishments in Canada and supplied 29 percent of manufacturing employment. They accounted for 34 percent of total wages and salaries paid in Canadian manufacturing in 1961, 40 percent of the value added by manufacturing, and 40 percent of the selling value of factory shipments. Of the total number of larger foreign-controlled establishments, those controlled in the United States formed 75 percent — 1,104 of the 1,464. The total group of larger foreign-controlled enterprises provided, on the average, more employment per establishment, higher wages and salaries, and a higher output per employee than the average for all manufacturing industry. The average number of employees per establishment was 254 for these larger foreign-controlled establishments, as against only 39 for all manufacturing establishments in Canada. Average salaries and wages per employee for the larger foreign-controlled establishments were 17 percent in excess of those for all manufacturing establishments. Value added by manufacture per employee was 36 percent greater for the former set of firms, while average selling value of factory shipments per employee was 37 percent greater. The averages are generally not very different as between the American-controlled and the total foreign-controlled of the larger manufacturing establishments. It should be repeated at this point that our comparisons between foreign-controlled and all manufacturing establishments in Canada overstate by some unknown amount the averages for the former compared with those for the latter, simply because the latter group includes not only firms with assets of $1 million or more, but *all* the smaller enterprises as well.

It is more meaningful, therefore, to concentrate on enterprises with aggregate investment of more than $25 million in Canada, since it is possible in this case to compare foreign-controlled with Canadian-controlled enterprises within the same broad size group. The data in Table 25 show that, in this size group in 1961, on the average, both the foreign-controlled enterprises as a whole and the American-controlled group alone had more employees, paid higher salaries and wages, and achieved a higher value added per employee and per establishment than was true of the resident-controlled enterprises. Thus the foreign-controlled enterprises with assets of $25 million or more averaged 13 percent more employees per establishment and 6.5 percent higher average salaries and wages per employee, while the average value added by manufacture was 13 percent greater per employee and fully 28 percent greater per establishment. More detailed data published by the Dominion Bureau of Statistics indicate that U.S.-controlled establishments in this size group had higher averages in each of the four respects noted than either their Canadian or U.K.-controlled counterparts. Establishments controlled in other foreign countries paid higher wages per employee and achieved a higher net product per employee than those controlled in the United States, the United Kingdom, and Canada. It may be added that the average investment per employee for enterprises with assets of $25 million or more was $22,100 for those controlled

TABLE 25

TOTALS AND AVERAGES PER ESTABLISHMENT AND PER EMPLOYEE FOR PRINCIPAL MANUFACTURING STATISTICS, LARGER FOREIGN-CONTROLLED ENTERPRISES AND ALL ENTERPRISES, 1961

		Manufacturing Enterprises by Aggregate Investment in Canada and by Location of Control										
		More than $25 Million and Controlled in					$1-25 Million and Controlled in		More than $1 Million and Controlled in		All Manufacturing Enterprises in Canada	Manufacturing [a]
		(1)	(2) All	(3)	(4) All	(5)÷(3)	(6)	(7) All	(8)	(9) All	(10)	(11)÷(10)
Item	Unit	U.S.	Foreign	Canada	Countries	(%)[a]	U.S.	Foreign	U.S.	Foreign		(%)
Establishments	No.	364	510	474	984	108	740	954	1,104	1,464	32,415	4.5
Total employees	'000	159	207	169	376	123	125	166	284	372	1,265	29
Average per establishment	No.	438	405	357	382	113	169	174	258	254	39	651
Total salaries and wages	$mil.	840	1,070	823	1,893	130	551	732	1,391	1,802	5,231	34
Average per establishment	$'000	2,308	2,099	1,735	1,924	121	774	767	1,260	1,231	161	765
Average per employee	$	5,270	5,177	4,863	5,036	106	4,403	4,417	4,889	4,839	4,136	117
Value added by manufacture	$mil.	2,086	2,568	1,860	4,428	138	1,327	1,699	3,413	4,267	10,682	40
Average per establishment	$'000	5,731	5,036	3,924	4,500	128	1,793	1,781	3,092	2,915	330	883
Average per employee	$	13,087	12,422	10,997	11,781	113	10,611	10,257	11,999	11,459	8,445	136
Selling value of factory shipments	$mil.	5,208	6,326	4,290	10,616	148	2,688	3,465	7,896	9,791	24,243	40
Average per establishment	$'000	14,306	12,404	9,050	10,788	137	3,632	3,632	7,152	6,688	748	894
Average per employee	$	32,668	30,598	25,360	28,241	121	21,498	20,915	27,758	26,291	19,165	137

[a] See qualification in text regarding ratios in columns (5) and (11).

Source: Dominion Bureau of Statistics, *The Canadian Balance of International Payments, 1963, 1964, and 1965*, Statement 71.

in the United States, $21,400 for those controlled in the United Kingdom, $144,000 for those controlled in other foreign countries, and $18,900 for manufacturing enterprises in this size group controlled in Canada.

In other words, if one concentrates on only the largest size category of firms and makes comparisons between the resident-owned and the foreign-owned, the resident-owned firms would appear to be smaller on average in terms of employees and shipments, with a lower capital intensity, and paying lower wages and salaries per employee. It should be added, however, that this conclusion could be held with more conviction if more detail on the size distribution of those firms with assets in excess of $25 million was available. There are some very large resident-owned and non-resident-owned firms in Canada, and these would have a very substantial effect on the arithmetic averages used; these arithmetic averages would be greatly affected by extreme values.

Another way to look at the question of relative size is through data reported under CALURA. The report for 1962 gives detail by size of firm (value of assets) for manufacturing companies.[2] This detail indicates that manufacturing companies whose stock was owned 50 percent or more abroad accounted for 13 percent of the total number of firms when assets were under $0.5 million, 24 percent when assets were $0.5 million to $0.9 million, 42 percent when they were $1.0 million to $4.9 million, and 57 percent when they were $5 million or more. Clearly, the foreign-owned manufacturing firms are more heavily concentrated towards the larger size range, at least by comparison with their resident-owned counterparts. It must be added, however, that the difference narrows considerably for the group with assets of $1 million and more.[3] These differences in size of firm may have important implications for the competitive ability of the firm, for reasons to be noted later in this section.

Another way to consider the efficiency of foreign-owned firms is to look at their *profitability*. It should be emphasized that the profits of firms may be an index not only of their efficiency, but also of the degree of competition in the system. Comparatively high profits may, in effect, reflect a lack of competition rather than superior efficiency of the firms concerned. Data on profitability by industry and by ownership were presented in an earlier section. It will be recalled that there did not appear to be a significant over-all difference in profitability of foreign-owned firms compared with resident-owned firms in the commodity-producing industries. The exception may be in secondary manufacturing, where the foreign-owned firms have somewhat higher profit rates than their resident-owned counterparts, particularly if profit rates are measured relative to sales rather than equity. It is not possible to be conclusive on this point, given only the available data, for reasons noted earlier.

---

[2] CALURA, *Report for 1962*, pp. 32, 83-86.

[3] The study by Safarian, which compares 96 resident-owned firms and 160 non-resident-owned firms with assets of $1 million or more, found that the difference between the two sets of firms in terms of size of assets was probably not significant statistically. It should be recalled that his data represent firms in industries where the two sets of firms co-exist, rather than all manufacturing industries as such (pages 267-69).

The data given in Table 26 compare, for 188 subsidiaries in Canada, the subsidiary's *unit costs of production* in 1959 relative to those of the parent, on major comparable products. For 57 percent of the subsidiaries, unit production costs were typically higher than those of the parent; in 20 percent, about the same; and in 11 percent, lower. In the remaining 12 percent, the unit cost varied or the products were not generally comparable. The larger firms showed a range of costs much closer to the parents'. Thus only 18 percent of those with assets of $25 million or more had unit costs in excess of the parent's, in contrast to 60 percent for each of the smaller size groups shown in the table. It should be

TABLE 26

UNIT PRODUCTION COSTS OF SUBSIDIARIES IN CANADA
RELATIVE TO THOSE OF THE PARENT ABROAD
ON MAJOR COMPARABLE PRODUCTS, 1959
(number of companies)

Subsidiary's Typical Unit Cost	Country of Control		Asset Size in $ Millions			
	U.S.	All Foreign	Under 1	1 - 4.9	5 - 24.9	25 & over
Higher than parent's	80	108	47	33	18	5
About the same	29	37	15	13	4	5
Lower than parent's	18	20	9	5	2	5
Varies	10	10	1	1	3	4
Not applicable	8	13	1	1	3	5
No response and not available	82	92	31	29	13	8
Total	227	280	104	82	43	35

Source: A..E. Safarian, *Foreign Ownership of Canadian Industry,* p. 203.

added that the largest size category of firms included many reporting either that their unit costs varied in relation to the parent's or that the products were not comparable. The same study also yields 103 observations on the precise difference in unit costs, with 59 companies indicating higher costs, 37 reporting unit costs about the same, and 7 with lower unit costs. For the 59 companies with higher costs, 21 reported that unit costs were no more than 10 percent higher than the parent's and 24 that unit costs were 11 to 20 percent higher. Only one-fourth of the 103 precise figures for unit-cost differences indicated that the subsidiary's costs were more than 16 percent above those of the parent. In brief, it would appear that where unit costs are higher, they are, in most cases, not much higher.

The only comprehensive study of unit costs in American firms and in their subsidiaries abroad, pertaining to the year 1960 (see Table 27), also indicates results similar to those noted: 51 percent of the subsidiaries in Canada showed higher costs than the parent; 29 percent, about the same; and 20 percent, lower. Only 24 percent had costs exceeding those of the parent by 16 percent or more.

Unit costs were typically lower than those of the parent for the subsidiaries in the United Kingdom and the Common Market. The Canadian subsidiary cost structure was better than that in Australia. While Latin America had a higher percentage than Canada of reporting subsidiaries in the lower-cost group, the spread from low to high was also greater.

TABLE 27

PERCENTAGE DISTRIBUTION OF FOREIGN TO DOMESTIC (U.S.)
TOTAL UNIT COSTS BY AREA AND CLASS INTERVAL, 1960
(percentages)

Foreign Subsidiary's Unit Costs Compared with Parent's in U.S.	Percentage of Each Area's Reporting Subsidiaries					
	Canada	U.K.	Common Market	Latin America	Australia	Other
Costs lower than U.S.	20	74	64	31	21	42
Costs as % of U.S. costs:						
Less than 55%	2	3	4	3	–	17
55 - 84%	4	52	44	18	16	8
85 - 94%	13	19	16	10	5	17
Costs same as U.S.	29	13	9	11	11	8
Costs higher than U.S.	51	13	27	58	68	50
Costs as % of U.S. costs:						
106 - 115%	27	6	11	8	11	8
116 - 145%	20	6	4	26	26	25
More than 145%	4	–	11	24	32	17
Total	100	100	100	100	100	100

Note: Component figures may not add precisely to totals owing to rounding.

Source: Theodore R. Gates and Fabian Linden, *Costs and Competition: American Experience Abroad,* National Industrial Conference Board, 1961, p. 13.

The major reason given for lower unit costs in Canada, where this occurred, was lower wage rates. Among the firms which reported higher unit costs, much the most important reason given was shorter production runs or lower volume in Canada — or that this led to less mechanization in Canada than was the case in the parent company. Other significant reasons given were that wage rates were higher in Canada (virtually all replies of this sort were from firms owned overseas), that duties on imports led to higher unit costs compared with the parent's, and that the subsidiary had higher costs for raw materials and components. It should be noted that almost half the observations for companies with higher unit costs concentrated on the first reason — namely, that production runs were shorter, volume was lower, or that these led to less mechanization. It is important to note that there does not appear to be much relationship between the age of the subsidiary and the level of its unit costs relative to the parent's. In other words, unit-cost differences tend to persist after the establishment of the subsidiary, partly because cost-reducing changes which might be applicable to the subsidiary would also in many cases be applicable to the parent as well. This suggests that the cost disadvantage of the subsidiaries relative to the parent will not disappear simply with time, but will require some fundamental changes in structure of industry.[4]

Structure of Industry, Tariffs, and Efficiency

The proximate cause of the relative inefficiency of subsidiary companies compared to the parent companies is evident if one looks at the structure of their production in Canada. The great majority of these firms are producing items in Canada which are very similar to those of their parents. Thus 59 percent of the respondents in Safarian's study indicated that the Canadian company was producing products generally identical to those of the affiliate, while 28 percent reported their products were only marginally different. In only 13 percent of these firms were the products substantially modified or not comparable. A majority in even the largest size group of firms (with assets of $25 million or more) reported their products to be, in the main, only marginally different from those of the affiliate.

Moreover, most of these firms are producing something close to the full product range of the parent company. In two-thirds of the cases the subsidiary was producing at least a majority of the parent's product items. In 8 percent of the subsidiaries, the products represented a wider range than those of the parent; in 31 percent, about the same range; and in 28 percent, a majority of the parent's product items were being produced. In each of the four size categories used in Table 28, it turned out that a majority of the firms were producing at least a majority of the parent's product items. Meanwhile, however, the subsidiary companies are, on average, much smaller than their foreign parents. Almost three-quarters of the Canadian firms reported that they were one-tenth or less the size of their foreign parent, and 28 percent of them reported they were only 5 or less percent of the parent's size. Even among the firms with assets of $25 million or more, fully 20 of the 35 reported they were one-tenth or less the size of the parent.[5]

The importance of these points will be evident if one recalls from the preceding sections that the absolute differences in size of firm and in structure, relative to the parent, have significant effects on the performance of the firm. A marked difference in almost every aspect of performance arises in relation to the absolute size of the firm, as noted under the various topics discussed earlier. In the asset-size categories of under $1 million, $1 million to $4.9 million, $5 million to $24.9 million, and $25 million and over, the medians for sales in Canada as a percentage of the subsidiary's total sales were 100, 100, 95, and 92,

---

[4] Safarian, *op. cit.*, pp. 202-09.
[5] *Ibid.*, pp. 211-13.

TABLE 28

COMPARISON OF PRODUCTS AND SIZE OF CANADIAN FIRM
RELATIVE TO THOSE OF ITS FOREIGN PARENT
(number of companies)

	All Firms	Asset Size in $ millions [a]			
		Under 1	1 - 4.9	5 - 24.9	25 and over
1. Nature of products compared with parent's					
Identical with comparable products of parent	156	66	51	16	16
Marginally different	73	27	20	13	9
Substantially modified	17	4	6	4	2
Not comparable	19	5	5	4	5
No reply	15	2	0	6	3
Total	280	104	82	43	35
2. Range of products compared with parent's					
Wider than parent's	20	7	8	3	2
About the same	79	29	34	4	9
Majority of parent's products	72	22	21	15	9
Minority of parent's products	37	18	6	6	3
Only a few	29	14	3	7	4
Not comparable, other	16	6	3	3	4
No response to question	27	8	7	5	4
Total	280	104	82	43	35
3. Percentage size relative to parent [b]					
1 - 5	67	27	21	9	7
6 - 10	105	44	30	15	13
11 - 15	20	4	10	4	1
16 - 20	21	8	6	3	2
Over 20	26	10	6	3	6
No response	41	11	9	9	6
Total	280	104	82	43	35

[a] Totals will not add to 280 because 16 firms could not be classified by size.

[b] The comparisons were usually given in either sales or assets.

Source: A. E. Safarian, *Foreign Ownership of Canadian Industry,* p. 212.

respectively; the medians for percentage of purchases in Canada were 70, 80, 80, and 85; and the medians for research and development as a percentage of sales were 0, 0, 0.23, and 0.23. For research and development as a percentage of sales, the third quartiles, by size category of firms, were 0.50, 1.00, 1.14, and 1.35. As was noted earlier, 65 percent of the firms with assets of over $1 million had a president who was a national of the country of the parent, as against 30 percent for firms with assets of $25 million or more. Fifty-five percent of the largest firms had one or more resident "outside" directors, i.e., directors not otherwise associated with the subsidiary or the parent, as compared with only 25 percent of the smallest firms.

The degree of specialization relative to the parent is also important. As was noted earlier, firms with a narrow range of products compared with the parent tend more often than firms with a wide range to sell part of their output abroad and to make a high proportion (90 to 100 percent) of their purchases in Canada. The percentage doing research and development does not show any clear pattern in relation to range of products. If one examines the data within size groups for the firms involved, in order to minimize the effect of size, the result is to strengthen the association between, on the one hand, range of products and, on the other, the sales and purchase behaviour just discussed. Finally, performance is also associated with the nature of the products compared with the parent. As the degree of differentiation of products from those of the parent increases, so too does the proportion of subsidiaries involved in exports and research.

If the foreign-owned firms in Canada suffer in terms of comparisons with the parent, it is likely that the resident-owned firms competing with them generally appear even less impressive in a number of aspects of performance. Data are not available to demonstrate this point in detail, but the logic of it will be clear if one reflects on some of the points made earlier. The foreign-owned firm can escape some of the problems of small scale because of the specialized commodities and services which, as demonstrated earlier, are available from the parent. The resident-owned firm must rely on specialized firms which are not related to it to supply these, or it must secure them by licensing agreement with unrelated firms. Barring these alternatives, it must be larger than its foreign-owned counterpart in order to achieve that scale of operations at which all economies of large-scale operation become available.[6] It was suggested earlier that the resident-owned firm in manufacturing may in fact be smaller than, or, in comparable industries, no larger than, its non-resident-owned counterpart. Thus there is a distinct possibility that unless other reasons exist, of a sort that would give superior efficiency to the resident-owned firm, its unit-cost position in production may be no better than that of the non-resident-owned firm.

To search still further for the explanation of the structure of industry noted above, one must examine the motives for direct investment in manufacturing in the first place. A detailed empirical study made in the 1930s concluded that the tariff was by far the most important reason for direct investment in Canadian

---

[6] See Stefan Stykolt and H. C. Eastman, "A Model for the Study of Protected Oligopolies," *Economic Journal*, June, 1960, pp. 336-47.

manufacturing.[7] Indeed, the study went on to suggest that "in the absence of tariffs the remaining barriers would be insufficient to explain the establishment of many — probably the majority — of the plants now in existence." Other significant factors were transportation economies and after-sales servicing. Among the subsidiaries that Safarian studied, about one-fifth of those established in Canada since World War II reported that the Canadian tariff was the major reason for their establishment. Another one-third indicated that the expansion of the Canadian market was a primary reason for their establishment, but some of the replies of this sort may well have been related also to the fact of tariff protection in the Canadian market. The tariff may be less important now than it was in the earlier periods in inducing direct investment into Canada, but it would be unwise to de-emphasize for even the present the role of the Canadian tariff and other barriers to trade in persuading firms abroad to locate in Canada rather than to export their products to Canada.

The relevance of this point to the question of efficiency is both direct and indirect. It is direct in the sense that firms induced by the tariff to locate in Canada are clearly not going to be as efficient in the first instance as the parent abroad; if they were as efficient, it would not be necessary to use tariff protection to bring them to Canada. It is quite true that, over time, the firm may reduce its costs in Canada relative to those of the parent, although, as noted above, there was not any simple *general* relationship between unit costs relative to the parent's and the passage of time. The tariff may also encourage the proliferation of products in the Canadian subsidiary as a means of compensating for the relatively small market in Canada. However, the tariff by itself would not be a sufficient explanation of the product proliferation and related relative inefficiency of Canadian industry, for the simple reason that firms which are competing do have the option of specializing production among themselves and relative to imports, and they can secure volume through this route. Such competition may both reduce the number of firms and increase their average size, but it should also lead to increases in the volume of output as a result of more specialization among the remaining firms.

This latter point about the structure of industry has been emphasized by a number of economists working in this area, who have pointed to the relationship of the Canadian tariff and of oligopolistic market structures to the inefficient scale of production. Their work has suggested strongly the need for reorganizing existing market structures through competitive forces — including tariff reduction and/or stronger anti-combines measures — as an important part of the attempt to increase the specialization of output and to reduce or eliminate the cost differentials between some aspects of Canadian industry and industry abroad. The findings of Safarian are relevant to these conclusions, in the sense of pointing to the relationship that improved performance and improved scale bear

---

[7]Herbert Marshall, Frank A. Southard, Jr., and Kenneth Taylor, *Canadian-American Industry* (New Haven: Yale University Press, 1936), p. 209.

to specialization and differentiation of products relative to those of the parent. [8] Finally, it should be noted that foreign tariffs and trade barriers, and particularly American tariffs, which discriminate against imports of manufactured products also affect the capacity of Canadian industry to compete efficiently with respect to exports of manufactures.

In emphasizing the importance of tariffs and other barriers to trade, and of imperfections of competition, we do not mean to exclude other factors which can be important in specific cases. Industry structures differ, and there is a need to recognize these differences when policies are developed. Moreover, an active anti-combines policy is not inconsistent with recognition of the fact that any rationalization program must permit mergers in some industries, along with greater specialization among firms. While this could raise serious problems of increased concentration of industry in a small market, it need not do so in the context of an open economy. Our general point is simply that it is difficult to see how the rationalization of Canadian industry for the sake of improved performance is possible without substantial reorganization of the structure of industry and, as a significant part of this process, further reduction of Canadian and foreign tariffs and an assurance that firms will take advantage of these.

It should be emphasized that firms producing primary products or engaged in primary manufacturing are generally in a strong position in relation to their parents, because their unit costs are the same as, or lower than, those of the parent or because the products are not comparable. Even among the firms engaged in secondary manufacturing, a significant portion — as much as one-third — have unit costs close to those of the parent. Moreover, there is already some specialization of production relative to the parent, as noted earlier. Nor is it always necessary to achieve a large volume of operations in order to secure minimum costs. Finally, some industries will remain domestic in orientation because of heavy transfer costs. The changes required for the rationalization of industrial structure will often be a matter of degree and direction of change, though they will require significant reorganization of production within and among firms in a number of industries in secondary manufacturing.

In conclusion, the emphasis of this section should be noted. Within the given structure of industry, many of the firms attracted to Canada are unlikely to be able to reduce their costs sufficiently in relation to the parent's as to be able to export significantly or to capture a larger share of the domestic market. Canadians have too often attempted to attract industry to the country by means of the tariff and other barriers to trade, in areas of manufacturing where such industry might not otherwise exist or might not come into being as soon, and have then expected the same firms to compete on the export market or to raise

---

[8] See the previous footnote reference to the article by Stykolt and Eastman and also the book by H. C. Eastman and S. Stykolt, *The Tariff and Competition in Canada* (Toronto: Macmillan, 1967). See also H. Edward English, *Industrial Structure in Canada's International Competitive Position* (Montreal: Canadian Trade Committee, 1964). For the relationship of oligopoly and foreign investment see Bernard Bonin, *L'investissement étranger à long terme au Canada*, Chap. 7.

their domestic content as if they were efficient by world standards. It makes more sense to attempt to achieve a more efficient structure of industry — by inducing relatively more Canadian resources into industries in which Canada has advantages or can develop them, and, in addition, by encouraging more specialization on the part of firms within such industries. Finally, it should be noted that while this section has emphasized the inefficiency of some foreign-owned firms relative to their parents, it has also emphasized the need for the causes of such relative inefficiency to be clear. The firms are not relatively inefficient because they are foreign-owned. The relative inefficiency often reflects the fact that legal or economic barriers to trade often require local production, while the demand and cost situation and other aspects of industry structure often do not permit fully efficient production. It was noted that the performance of resident-owned firms does not appear to be better and, in some cases, may be worse.

The United Kingdom's Experience with American-Owned Subsidiaries

An important similarity between the United Kingdom's and Canada's experience is that 68 percent of the 205 U.S. affiliates in U.K. manufacturing examined by Dunning replied that their end products were comparable in all major respects with those of the American parent. There was a modification to this in that 74 percent of these firms noted minor or marginal differences in the products because of specialized market tastes and needs. Fully 150 firms, or 75 percent of the total sample, said that their product range was narrower in the United Kingdom than it was in the United States — a larger proportion of firms than was the case in Canada. It should be added that within any particular product group the number of models manufactured — the number of sizes, styles, and so on — was often greater.[9] Dunning also goes on to note that, of the 140 firms that reported on their costs of production relative to those of the parent, only 21 said their costs were higher than in the United States, 36 said their costs were about the same, and 83 said they were lower. It was possible to get more precise estimates for 40 of the lower-cost firms. In eight cases the firms were able to produce at below half the parent's unit costs; in 12, at between one-half and three-quarters; and in 20, at between 80 percent and 90 percent of the parent's cost. Costs in the United Kingdom tended to be higher than in the United States in the mass-production-type of industries in which heavy capital-ization was required, and to be lower where the proportion of value added by labour was highest. Dunning notes that subsidiaries pay only a small part of the research and development and overhead expenses of the parent, thus reducing their costs while making considerable use of the parent's facilities. He also points out that the subsidiary was often able to sell in export markets at prices below those of the parent and that, in some cases, the parent had decided to serve all its overseas markets from the U.K. subsidiary.[10] It was noted earlier that the export performance of American manufacturing affiliates in the United Kingdom was considerably better than that of similar affiliates in Canada.

---

[9] Dunning, *American Investment in British Manufacturing Industry*, pp. 115-17.
[10] *Ibid.*, pp. 151-52.

Another study by Dunning, involving 50 American-owned firms and data for the year 1961, shows further comparisons with parent firms. Only 11 of the 50 subsidiaries had a higher volume of net output per worker than the parent. The most frequent reason given for this difference in productivity was the smaller scale of the U.K. operations, which permitted less mechanization. In all but six cases, however, the subsidiaries in the United Kingdom claimed that their unit manufacturing costs were lower than the parent's. Dunning also found that the productivity of a selection of American-owned firms was 18 percent above that of their British competitors. He suggests, using rather broad industry groups, that this difference reflects superior efficiency rather than the industrial composition of the two groups.[11]

Situation in Australia

Brash notes that the most important single reason given for investing in Australia was a desire to take advantage of the expected growth of the Australian market. He adds, however, that in the absence of barriers to trade, the expanding market might well be served by the United States through exports, possibly in cooperation with after-sales service supplied by a local company. Virtually all the other reasons given by the firms in his study have to do in one way or another with obstacles to trade — tariff barriers imposed by Australia being by far the most important of these. Indeed, one-half of all the respondent companies explicitly claimed that the desire to get around the Australian tariff was a motive for establishing there. Various other types of import controls were also important. In the Brash study as in others, it appears that manufacturing firms often invest abroad not so much to take advantage of differential prospects for profits in various countries, but to try to keep an actual or prospective export market which they can no longer serve through exports, because of tariff or other trade barriers.[12]

Comparing physical output per man year, Brash found that productivity was lower in Australia than in the United States in most of the cases for which he could get evidence. The main reason was the relatively small volume of production and the effect of this on methods of production. He secured 82 comparisons of unit costs of production as between the subsidiary and the parent. In 23 of these, Australian costs were below American; in 12, about the same; and in 47, higher. Where unit costs were higher than those in the United States, the range of costs relative to the American was higher than was evident for Canada, as noted earlier for the Canadian case. Again, the most important reason for lower Australian costs, where these were reported, was the relative cheapness of Australian labour. The most frequent reason for higher costs, as in the case of Canada, was the relatively low volume of production and the consequent underutilization of machinery or lower degree of mechanization. Brash notes that the value of production per person employed, for the factories in his sample of American-affiliated firms, was about 36 percent higher than in

[11] Dunning, *The Role of American Investment in the British Economy*, pp. 136-37, 143-44.

[12] Brash, *op. cit.*, pp. 35-40.

Australian industry generally; the higher output per person was the case in 8 of the 10 industries he examined. He suggests that the differences between American-affiliated and other Australian firms may reflect, in part, a difference in the size of firm and, in part, the use of modern techniques of management and production in American-affiliated firms, so that labour productivity would be higher even if capital-labour ratios were the same. In fact, however, machinery per employee appears to be higher for American-affiliated firms.[13]

---

[13] *Ibid.*, Chap. 7.

8

Performance and the Problem of Extraterritoriality

The analysis in the previous six chapters has been based on the assumption that the officers of the foreign-owned firms and of their parent companies have been acting in response to their private motivations in making decisions. The data which have been presented above essentially reflect the outcome of such private decisions made within the context of Canadian and foreign laws and policy principles which, until recently, were not specifically directed to the operations of foreign-owned firms. Increasingly in recent years, however, the operations of the foreign subsidiaries have been affected by government actions specifically designed to change the pattern of their performance. This is a complex and controversial subject which deserves a major study of its own. But some of the issues will be outlined here, particularly insofar as they relate to the performance of subsidiary firms.[1]

Extraterritorial Effects of U.S. Laws and Regulations

The problem is usually referred to broadly as that of extraterritoriality — that is, the extraterritorial effects of foreign laws and regulations on subsidiary operations in Canada. The known cases to date in Canada have involved attempts through U.S. laws and regulations to determine certain transactions of subsidiary companies. Among the issues these attempts have raised, particular prominence

---

[1] For further comments on the issues raised here, see Kingman Brewster, Jr., *Law and United States Business in Canada* (Montreal and Washington: Canadian-American Committee, 1960); Safarian, *op. cit.*, pp. 144-46, 166-67, 253-56; and Report of the Task Force on the Structure of Canadian Industry, *Foreign Ownership and the Structure of Canadian Industry* (Ottawa: Queen's Printer, 1968), pp. 310-46.

has been received by those of trade with certain third countries, anti-trust policy, and remedial measures for balance of payments problems.

The United States has long had a number of laws and regulations to control trade by its citizens with Communist countries so as to serve her foreign-policy objectives, including those related to national security. Among these laws and regulations are the Foreign-Assets Control regulations of the U.S. Treasury, which prohibit trade with Communist China, North Korea, North Vietnam, and (with some qualifications) Cuba. The regulations also make parent companies in the United States responsible for preventing sales of goods to these countries from their foreign subsidiaries, under penalty of prosecution of the officers of the parent firm when violations occur. The object is to prevent the force of the regulations, as they apply to residents of the United States, from being frustrated through trade by American-owned subsidiaries abroad.

Canadian policy, by contrast, generally permits trade with these countries except for exports of strategic goods. This difference in policy has led to serious conflicts of interest for some American-owned subsidiaries in Canada. Attempts have been made to work out a solution, notably as reflected in the 1958 Eisenhower-Diefenbaker Joint Statement on Export Policies. This involved formal annual consultations on this and some other matters and the possibility of case-by-case exemptions that would permit subsidiaries in Canada to export to such countries under certain conditions. Little is known about how well this approach has worked in practice. Indeed, little is known publicly about the over-all economic or political ramifications of the whole question. It has been apparent, however, that the alleged cases of refusals to export which have come to public notice have aroused widespread and generally critical comment in Canada.[2]

The application of U.S. anti-trust law and policy has also, on occasion, raised questions which border on extraterritoriality. These have arisen particularly in attempts by the U.S. government and courts to assure competition in the United States through provisions on trade with other countries, including the ways in which American-owned subsidiaries abroad operate. Controversy over these cases has, in turn, led to provisions for joint consultation, or for at least notification, where the interests of the other country are affected by the enforcement of anti-trust or anti-combines policies. This is unlikely to be a permanent solution so long as the Canadian and the American approaches to such policies differ in some important respects.

A related issue arose over the implementation of U.S. balance of payments policies.[3] The sizable U.S. deficit has been a matter of general concern for a decade. Some issues of particular concern to Canada, a major capital importer,

---

[2] See, for example, the instances noted in the article by Walter Stewart in the *Star Weekly*, February 5, 1966, pp. 2-4.

[3] For a detailed analysis of the nature and consequences of these policies as they related to Canada, see Sperry Lea, *Canada and the U.S. Capital Restraint Programs* (Montreal and Washington: Canadian-American Committee, forthcoming).

have appeared since the Interest Equalization Tax of 1963, the first of many U.S. measures to moderate the outflow of U.S. dollar funds and to otherwise alter foreign investment and lending to favour the U.S. payments record. Canada obtained an exemption from the Interest Equalization Tax with respect to new borrowing, in return for establishing as a ceiling its then existing level of foreign exchange reserves. In March, 1965, the first of a series of voluntary restraint programs was introduced for U.S. financial and business institutions. Canada was included in the goal of repatriating short-term funds from abroad where possible. But Canada was given priority in the guidelines which limited new lending abroad and was exempted at this time from restraints on U.S. direct investment.

A few months later, however, the direct investment guidelines were revised to include Canada in the global arithmetic. Each U.S. parent company was permitted a specified annual increase in its world level of "direct investment" in developed countries, a phrase defined to include not merely new outflows of U.S. dollars but also retained subsidiary earnings typically destined for reinvestment. Canada's inclusion for the year 1966 was justified by the U.S. authorities mainly by the view that the previous exemption had led to increased direct investment flows to Canada, much of which represented funds "flowing through" to other countries covered by the guidelines.

A key Canadian objection to the 1966 guidelines was that the U.S. parents and subsidiaries would now be required to make, for other than economic reasons, decisions affecting Canadian operations. From the Canadian standpoint, the U.S. parent companies were seen as being urged (1) to curtail direct investment flows to Canada and/or increase the repatriation of subsidiary earnings, whose reinvestment role was now to be taken by increased borrowing in the Canadian capital market; and (2) to raise exports of components and raw materials from U.S. sources to their Canadian firms, while moderating subsidiary exports to the United States. In such ways, private economic decision-making was to serve directly the official objectives of U.S. balance of payments policy. If successful, the result would be not simply to worsen the Canadian balance of payments, but also, in effect, to make a substantial segment of the Canadian business community directly responsive to U.S. policy in these respects — through the medium of the parent-subsidiary relationship — and correspondingly less responsive to those Canadian policies whose effects conflicted with the U.S. need to remedy its payments record.

The official Canadian response to the U.S. controls on capital outflows was varied. Both the Bank of Canada and the Department of Finance, for example, took steps to discourage new borrowing in Canada by U.S. subsidiaries — borrowing prompted by that element of the guidelines encouraging such firms to look elsewhere than in the United States for funds. Canadian objections to the guidelines affecting parent-subsidiary operations led to a statement issued as a result of a meeting of the Canada-United States Joint Committee on Trade and Economic Affairs in March, 1966. The statement said in part:

> The U.S. members made clear that the U.S. government was not requesting U.S. corporations to induce their Canadian subsidiaries to act in any way that differed from their normal business practices as regards the repatriation of earnings, purchasing and sales policies, or their other financial and commercial policies.

This appeared to exempt Canada from the guidelines legislation on direct investment, but no formal exemption was made.

At the end of March, 1966, the government of Canada issued to subsidiary companies in Canada a set of guiding principles indicating what was expected of them in terms of good corporate practice. In addition, data were collected for the first time on certain aspects of subsidiary performance — such as on exports and imports and on selected quarterly capital transactions — from the larger and medium-size firms. This set of "counter-guidelines" will be considered shortly.

On the first day of 1968 the United States introduced a "Program of Action" with a stiffer and now mandatory regulation on direct investment flows, including those to Canada. This could not have come at a worse time from Canada's point of view. The world monetary situation was tense after the devaluation of the pound sterling in November. The domestic economic situation early in 1968 required a fine handling of Canadian monetary and fiscal policy, quite apart from any internal political difficulties. The U.S. move, though originally judged by spokesmen for both governments to promise no ill effects, turned out to complicate the situation seriously, not least because some firms in Canada (including direct investment firms) apparently misinterpreted the eventual effects on the Canadian balance of payments and unnecessarily speeded payments abroad. There occurred a significant loss of reserves and strong pressure on the Canadian dollar. This was no doubt the key reason for a Canadian-American agreement in March (the Sharp-Fowler letters were exchanged on March seventh) to exempt Canada entirely from all but one of the various balance of payments regulations affecting U.S. lending and investment. [4] In return, Canada agreed to establish guidelines and a reporting system for her institutions so as to ensure that Canada would not be used as a "pass-through" to other countries in a way that would frustrate the U.S. program. In effect, the cost of exemption was surveillance of capital exports from Canada to third countries.

The Canadian Guiding Principles

In view of the emphasis in this study on the performance of subsidiary firms, it is of interest to look more closely at the Canadian guiding principles to subsidiaries. Such guiding principles of good corporate practice have been mentioned publicly by Canadian government officials, among others, for at least a decade. The guidelines were issued at the end of March, 1966, to larger and medium-size subsidiaries. The timing, as noted, was related to the application of mandatory guidelines to Canada by the U.S. authorities. The long-term purpose was to make the firms aware in a general way of desirable patterns of performance, as seen by the Canadian government, in the hope that these would be built into their operations as conditions warranted. At the same time, the

---

[4] The Interest Equalization Tax was still retained on outstanding issues of Canadian securities. It should be added that the ceiling on Canada's foreign exchange reserves is no longer a fixed figure and that Canada has agreed to keep such reserves in a form which improves the recorded U.S. deficit.

Canadian government began to collect data from these firms on a continuing and confidential basis, on some aspects of their operations.

The guiding principles are given below:

1. Pursuit of sound growth and full realization of the company's productive potential, thereby sharing the national objective of full and effective use of the nation's resources.

2. Realization of maximum competitiveness through the most effective use of the company's own resources, recognizing the desirability of progressively achieving appropriate specialization of productive operations within the internationally affiliated group of companies.

3. Maximum development of market opportunities in other countries as well as in Canada.

4. Where applicable, to extend processing of natural resource products to the extent practicable on an economic basis.

5. Pursuit of a pricing policy designed to assure a fair and reasonable return to the company and to Canada for all goods and services sold abroad, including sales to the parent company and other foreign affiliates.

6. In matters of procurement, to search out and develop economic sources of supply in Canada.

7. To develop as an integral part of the Canadian operation wherever practicable, the technological, research, and design capability necessary to enable the company to pursue appropriate product-development programs so as to take full advantage of market opportunities domestically and abroad.

8. Retention of a sufficient share of earnings to give appropriate financial support to the growth requirements of the Canadian operation, having in mind a fair return to shareholders on capital invested.

9. To work towards a Canadian outlook within management through purposeful training programs, promotion of qualified Canadian personnel, and inclusion of a major proportion of Canadian citizens on its board of directors.

10. To have the objective of a financial structure which provides opportunity for equity participation in the Canadian enterprise by the Canadian public.

11. Periodically to publish information on the financial position and operations of the company.

12. To give appropriate attention and support to recognized national objectives and established government programs designed to further Canada's eco-

nomic development and to encourage and support Canadian institutions directed towards the intellectual, social, and cultural advancement of the community.

The communications sent to the Canadian subsidiaries on the subject of the guiding principles clearly recognized that there was already widespread adherence to these principles among the subsidiaries in Canada, but added that there was room for improvement where the principles were not already applied.

Statements of this kind, designed to cover a wide variety of situations, must necessarily be general in tone. Some of the guiding principles are unnecessarily so, with a consequent loss of clarity. Thus, to urge a company to pursue sound growth does not specify what one has in mind; presumably no company would deliberately pursue what it recognized, within its own terms of reference, to be unsound or insufficient growth. Principle 1 should be related explicitly and closely to principles 2 and 3, which concern maximum competitiveness and specialization. This set of points should be spelled out to indicate clearly that the Canadian interest is for the subsidiary to secure a reduced number of product lines in Canada (along with securing the related research and some other overheads) to be developed for the domestic and international markets, rather than simply to proliferate on a small-volume basis all or most of the parent company's products. Again, it cannot be too meaningful to many companies to urge them to extend their processing of natural resource products to the extent practicable on an economic basis. Presumably companies already extend processing to the extent practicable on an economic basis, as they themselves understand these terms.

Similarly, principle 5 suggests that the companies pursue a pricing policy designed to assure a fair and reasonable return to the company and to Canada for all goods and services sold abroad, including sales to the parent company and other foreign affiliates. What may be fair and reasonable from the standpoint of an international company attempting to minimize its over-all tax burden may not be fair and reasonable from the standpoint of Canada. What is actually desired here is that, for purposes of taxation, goods and services sold between affiliates in different countries be placed on an arm's-length basis, the prices in this arm's-length basis being decided, where possible, by market prices for comparable goods and services; and where no such prices exist, they should be decided in consultation with the Canadian tax authorities. This would ensure that Canada secured her appropriate share of tax revenue from the sale of such goods and services. It should be noted that Canada could lose something in this process if the firms carried it to the logical conclusion, because many of the subsidiaries would be charged at market prices for services now secured for less than market prices or for no explicit payment at all from the foreign affiliate. The Canadian interest would then require that no more than an arm's-length price be paid for imported goods and services. The implications of these points were discussed at the end of the section on research and development.

The same question can be raised with respect to principle 6, which states that, in matters of procurement, subsidiaries are to search out and develop economic sources of supply in Canada. What may be economic to the international firm may or may not be economic from the standpoint of developing efficient sources of supply in Canada.

It is not entirely surprising that virtually all the firms indicated, in most of these respects, that they conformed or agreed with the principle enunciated — the terminology itself would lead to such a result for reasons already noted. On the other hand, for principle 7, which concerns the development of technical research, a significant minority of the firms indicated that they did not conform. In addition, most of the firms did not conform and a significant minority did not agree with the quite specific principles 10 and 11 regarding stock issue and reporting.

It will be admitted that the principles were issued in a situation where relatively little was known about the performance of the firms. Now that information is being collected regularly and other studies are available, the principles might be reviewed with the purpose of making them clearer and more specific. In addition, now that the firms have indicated their views in detail on the guiding principles, the review should ascertain whether the present phrasing is in all cases relevant and whether each guiding principle, as phrased, is in the Canadian interest. Sometimes Canada has a dual and conflicting interest in a specific principle — as witness the tendency for specialization within the international firm, if it means more vertical integration, to lead in some cases to more-centralized supervision of the subsidiary.

9

Conclusions[1]

Canadians have been concerned that the influence of the parent in the decision-making process of the subsidiary, where it is directed towards maximizing the profit of the international firm as a whole, may not lead to the maximum development or use of Canadian facilities or personnel. A definitive analysis of this point is impossible because one can only speculate on how Canada might have developed had there been less foreign direct investment. Even an analysis limited to the record of firms as they now exist is severely hampered by the lack of adequate data. But the data and the analyses which are available, inadequate although they may be, suggest that Canadians may have been worrying too much about certain things and not enough about others.

The most important observation about the performance of the subsidiaries is how varied it is. Sweeping generalized criticisms simply do not stand up under even cursory examination of the available data. More fundamentally, where behaviour that has been defined as undesirable by public authorities does appear, it often can be related closely to aspects of the economic environment in which the firm operates, but only distantly, or not at all, to the fact of foreign ownership as such. To be sure, some problems do arise specifically because of foreign ownership, and these will be noted shortly. But many of the economic aspects of performance that have concerned Canadians can be related more convincingly to industrial policy, or the lack of policy, in Canada and abroad.

The Determinants of Performance

What are some of the proximate determinants of the performance of subsidiaries in Canada which are noted in this study?

[1] Portions of this section are drawn and adapted from Safarian, *op. cit.*, Chap. 10.

A major one is the size of the firm. Medium-size and larger firms perform better, by the stated Canadian criteria, than smaller ones, by showing a greater number of Canadian nationals among the officers, more resident directors, a greater degree of the decision-making, a higher percentage of sales abroad, a lower percentage of purchases abroad, a greater proportion doing research (though not necessarily relatively more research among those doing it), a better cost position relative to the parent's, and a larger proportion with a minority stock issue (though firms in all size groups perform poorly in this respect).

In addition, for the criterion of nationality of presidents and resident directors, better performance is generally shown by firms which have a minority share issue and are less supervised by their foreign parents.

Better performance in such respects as higher exports and research, a smaller proportion of imports in purchases, and smaller unit-cost differences tends, on the other hand, to be associated with type of business: specifically, primary industries, including primary manufacturing, perform better by these tests, except that research is more highly concentrated in certain areas of secondary manufacturing.

Better performance is also associated with type of products, in that subsidiaries whose products are different from (or modified versions of) those made by the parent are more likely to satisfy the Canadian criteria.

Finally, better performance is also shown by firms whose product range is narrower than the parent's, except that, where the product range is very narrow and there is much vertical integration, the firms are also likely to receive more supervision from the parent than are those with a wider product range.

More fundamentally, the unsatisfactory performance of many foreign-owned firms can be traced to the economic circumstances which led to their establishment and to the inhibiting effects of continuing environmental factors. The standards of performance demanded by Canadians from many firms are impossible to achieve *within the given structure of Canadian industry*. It is futile to exhort a firm to export if its cost structure inhibits this or if it has to penetrate formidable foreign barriers to trade. A firm which has just located in Canada to get behind the Canadian tariff can hardly be expected to show an outstanding performance in exports or a high domestic content, at least in the beginning and perhaps indefinitely.

One can generalize these and other points by use of data on the structure of industry and on the motives of many firms for locating in Canada. Most subsidiaries in Canada produce close to the full range of the parent's products, while their size is generally only 5 to 10 percent of that of the parent. Their unit costs are typically higher than those of the parent on major comparable products, though usually not much higher. These characteristics can be partly traced to the Canadian tariff, which has been important in attracting manufacturing subsidiaries to Canada and in leading to an uneconomic proliferation of products and firms. The cost difference also reflects, in part, a lack of competition behind the tariff, competition which would lead to fewer and larger firms and more specialization among them. In addition, foreign barriers to trade reduce the size of the market for some firms located in Canada.

If one compares the larger foreign-owned firms in Canada with their resident-owned counterparts in broadly comparable industries, it is clear that economic performance is more closely related to other variables than it is to country of ownership. The foreign-owned firms may, of course, be expected to have a considerable number of nationals of the parent country in their executive ranks and boards, to rely on the parent for part of their funds, and to pay abroad much more in dividends and service charges. In broadly comparable circumstances, however, they do not appear to differ significantly in terms of either exports or research performed in Canada. The foreign-owned firm does import more than its resident-owned counterpart, but not markedly more. (Foreign-owned firms *as a whole* are better represented in export-oriented and research-oriented industries, and probably in import-oriented industries also, but this is clearly another matter since very different types of industry, size of firm, and other variables are involved in this comparison.) In brief, it would appear that both resident-owned and foreign-owned firms may have an equally unsatisfactory performance in terms of some of the key standards set by Canadian public authorities in recent years.

The foreign-owned firm in Canada is generally less efficient than its parent. It was noted, for example, that its unit cost of production is typically higher than its parent's on major comparable products. Moreover, its research and development expenditures are a smaller portion of sales and involve much less fundamental research. Such differences are attributable to a substantial extent to variations in size of firm, in degree of specialization by plant, and in consequent methods of production. These variations, in turn, relate to the above-noted problems of industrial structure in Canada. That the direct investment firm's performance varies with its environment can also be seen from British and Australian experience with American direct investment in their manufacturing industries. In the United Kingdom such firms are highly export- and research-oriented — more so than resident-owned British firms and also more so than American direct investment firms in Canadian and Australian manufacturing. By contrast, Australian experience to date appears to show lower levels of exports, and possibly of research as well, than is true of American firms in Canada. In part these differences can be traced to such private and public environmental factors as the different cost situations facing these subsidiaries in different countries and different degrees of public support for research.

Broader Economic Implications

Several broader points are raised by the conclusions of this study.

First, if we are correct in emphasizing the structure of industry as determined by private circumstance and public law, rather than ownership *per se*, then changes in that structure should improve performance. These changes can be defined precisely only in terms of the situation in each separate industry, but their general nature is clear: to rationalize industrial structure in the direction of more scale, more specialization, and more differentiation of product lines relative to the parent's — all in relation to a larger market including exports. Canada needs a more explicit strategy on industrial policy, spelled out not only in general terms, but also in a specific and integrated way that encompasses commercial policy, anti-combines policy, taxation policies, government support for research, and other aids to industry. Elements of this strategy already exist. In terms of the requirements of an efficient and expanding manufacturing sector, particular attention should be given to the development of efficient exports, efficient import substitution, and their relationship to research and development.[2]

The second point relates to the first. The gains from direct foreign investment can accrue in various ways — such as to the receipient country in the form of lower prices and better services than would otherwise be possible, to the parent firm in the form of greater after-tax profits, or to both in the form of the firm's superior performance in various other respects. The data presented in this paper suggest that the performance of the subsidiary firm, despite some competitive advantages it has, is generally no better than that of its resident-owned counterpart in roughly comparable circumstances. Inappropriate industrial policies may well have prevented Canada from maximizing the gains from foreign direct investment, as well as from Canadian investment.

Third, this emphasis on the environmental factors should not lead one to assume that there are no special characteristics attributable to foreign ownership as such. There are, in fact, costs to be minimized and benefits to be maximized; and Canada in particular, with her large foreign-owned sector, has much to gain from learning how to achieve these objectives. There are problems that arise specifically from foreign direct investment, such as the informal arrangements that exist within some international firms for restricting markets among their affiliates, and the need to minimize income paid abroad. The problems raised by extraterritorial extension of foreign law and policy through subsidiaries abroad require urgent and careful attention, because they present real and serious issues for both governments and international firms. There are advantages which Canadians can learn, and are learning, to exploit more fully — such as having access to certain kinds of research from the parent while developing other kinds within the subsidiary, or various benefits related to market contacts abroad — particularly as Canadian industry becomes more specialized. The question of the degree of decision-making exercised by the officers of the subsidiary will loom larger as rationalization of industry proceeds, since specialization, if it involves integration with the parent, may reduce the decision-making role of the subsidiary's officers in such areas as marketing.

Fourth, the kinds of changes envisaged here clearly imply the need for an alert and informed opinion, both private and public. The restructuring of

---

[2] On the links between exports and research and development in particular, see William Gruber *et al.*, "The R & D Factor in International Trade and International Investment of United States Industries," *The Journal of Political Economy*, February, 1967, and B. W. Wilkinson, *Canada's International Trade: An Analysis of Recent Trends and Patterns*, Chaps. 6 and 7.

Canadian industry and the maximization of the net gain from foreign investment involve major decisions by both private and public authorities. These are much more likely to succeed if the objectives are clear and realistic and if the relevant data and studies are available.

Fifth, we should emphasize again that the present study attempts a thorough analysis only for one major aspect of foreign corporate investment, namely, the industrial performance of firms. No attempt has been made to analyze systematically such matters as balance of payments effects, political effects, or over-all benefits and costs, all of which deserve fuller examination. [3] Nor have we dealt with a closely related question increasingly being raised in Canada — that of the apparent inability of Canadians themselves to undertake a larger proportion of Canadian business ventures. This raises complex questions about, among other things, how to improve Canadian organizational, financial, technological, and other skills. The reform of industrial structure discussed here may well be a key element in improving these skills and thereby in helping to enable Canadians to achieve greater participation in their country's industry.

Some Political Questions

Decisions made within the international firms are one thing, while attempts by governments to extend their laws and regulations abroad through subsidiaries are another. The extraterritorial extension of laws and regulations has both economic and political repercussions. The economic performance of subsidiary companies can be affected over time by direct pressures from governments, leading to results which will differ from those that such firms would achieve if they were acting independently of such pressures. Since such effects can be deleterious to the host country, the latter may try to countervail them by direct pressures of its own on the subsidiaries. Along with the intergovernmental tensions, the subsidiaries will be faced with a difficult conflict of loyalties.

The larger political aspects have raised more-serious concern in Canada. Many Canadians are wondering how far these issues may involve reduction of Canadian sovereignty — in the sense of reduced jurisdiction over resident corporations — and Canadian independence — in the sense of reduced capacity to implement distinctive policies.

Any over-all consideration of these issues must recognize that there are also positive political aspects to the process of foreign investment, such as those that stem from the increased economic power of the recipient country. Moreover, independence is not an absolute to be necessarily maximized under all circumstances in an increasingly interdependent world. That is, the maximum degree of independence may not necessarily be the optimum one, once the full economic and non-economic costs of any given degree of independence have been considered.

---

[3] For an analysis of other major aspects, see Report of the Task Force on the Structure of Canadian Industry, *Foreign Ownership and the Structure of Canadian Industry* (Ottawa: Queen's Printer, 1968).

These and related issues raise complex questions requiring much more consideration than they have yet received. But three points may be suggested in the present context. First, Canadians have demonstrated a clear desire to maintain some degree of independence in policy, in the sense of a sufficient capacity to undertake initiatives at home and abroad. These initiatives will not always correspond to those of closely allied countries. Second, the large and growing degree of interdependence among countries that develops through the medium, among others, of the foreign-owned firm is likely to continue to raise troublesome questions of the types noted here. Third, if mutually satisfactory methods of dealing with these issues are not worked out by multilateral or bilateral agreement among countries, the stakes may eventually be considered sufficiently important that governments will resort to unilateral and second-best solutions. The outcome may contribute to determining not only the room for independent initiatives left to national policies as interdependence grows, but also the future role of foreign direct investment.

APPENDIX
The Nature of the Available Data

The data available for the examination of the performance of foreign-owned firms and, indeed, of Canadian-owned firms as well are extremely limited. Much of the data was collected for other purposes and can only with difficulty be adapted to the purposes of the present study. A brief comment on the nature of the data will serve to warn the reader of the limitations of the present study. It might be added that comprehensive empirical studies of this subject are all too few in number.[1]

1. The Dominion Bureau of Statistics has published three surveys of the manufacturing operations of Canadian companies controlled in the United States and having assets of $1 million or more. The surveys cover the years 1946, 1953, and 1961. The last of these includes all foreign-controlled firms, and not only American-controlled firms, with assets of $1 million or more. The data cover number of employees, salaries and wages, materials used, value added, and value of products or shipments. Because of the exclusion of smaller firms, it is not possible to compare directly, in these various respects, foreign-controlled enterprises with Canadian-controlled enterprises.

2. Under the Corporations and Labour Unions Returns Act (CALURA), statistics are being collected concerning corporations whose gross revenues exceed $500,000 or whose assets exceed $250,000. Certain companies are excluded from the provisions of the Act, notably the chartered banks and most of the insurance companies operating in Canada. Data are supplied on the assets, equity, sales, and profits of the firms involved, by degree of foreign ownership and by some other characteristics. In addition, data are supplied on various types of payments abroad and on the characteristics of the managers and directors of the larger companies. This information is available for about 25,000 corporations, both resident-owned and non-resident-owned, for the years 1962, 1963, and 1964 on a detailed industry basis. A limited amount of information about specific companies is also available under the terms of the Act.

3. When the government of Canada decided early in 1966 to issue guiding principles to foreign-owned firms operating in Canada, the questionnaires, covering the years 1964 and 1965, were sent out to larger foreign-owned firms with assets in excess of $5 million. Replies were received in time for publication from 266 firms. Another 28 replies were not detailed enough to publish, 63 were received too late for publication or were promised for too

---

[1] Until 1967 the only postwar economic studies of the performance of foreign-owned subsidiaries in Canada were Irving Brecher and S.S. Reisman, *Canada-United States Economic Relations*, Royal Commission on Canada's Economic Prospects, 1957, and John Lindeman and Donald Armstrong, *Policies and Practices of United States Subsidiaries in Canada* (Montreal and Washington: Canadian-American Committee, 1961).

late a date, and 6 firms apparently refused to cooperate. The questionnaires requested, in some cases for the first time officially in Canada, data on the exports, imports, research expenditure, and income and service payments abroad of foreign-owned firms. Data on selected quarterly capital transactions by these companies have also been collected, partly in order to ascertain what the effects of the American and Canadian guidelines may have been on the international operations of these companies. The companies involved account for about one-third of the sales of all mining and manufacturing companies in Canada and about twice that proportion for all foreign-owned firms in these industries. Equivalent data on resident-owned firms are not available. Moreover, since valuation, classification, and timing for the data are not always consistent with other official data, comparisons with other series are still further limited.

4. The U.S. Department of Commerce has for some years published extensive data on the operations of American subsidiaries abroad. A complete census on the operations of such companies was carried out for the year 1957, covering the value of investments, exports and imports of subsidiary companies, local sales and purchases, earnings abroad, sources and uses of funds, and some other topics. For more recent years, the Department of Commerce has published some of the data on a sample basis, covering exports and imports of subsidiary companies, financing and sales of foreign affiliates of U.S. firms, and capital expenditures abroad. A second complete census is now under way. For comprehensiveness and detail, these official data have not been matched by any other country.

5. The most detailed private statistical study of Canadian experience in recent years is that of A. E. Safarian, *Foreign Ownership of Canadian Industry*. This study was based on interviews and questionnaires covering experience in the year 1959 or, in some cases, for an average of the late fifties. The 280 foreign-owned firms involved in the study accounted for between 9 and 12 percent of all firms owned by non-residents in the manufacturing, mining, and petroleum industries and for about 40 percent of the total assets of all such firms in these industries. The firms involved are biased towards the larger and medium-size firms and towards manufacturing. The study also includes comparisons with 96 resident-owned firms in industries in which resident-owned firms and non-resident-owned firms both exist. The 96 resident-owned firms had assets of $1 million or more each and were compared with 160 non-resident-owned firms each having assets of $1 million or more. The study covers the nature of management and of the control exercised by the parent, exports and imports, research and development, and the financing of the firms involved. Its advantage, compared with the ones listed above, is that it was designed specifically to answer the kinds of questions about performance that have attracted attention in recent years and is far more detailed, in terms of the topics covered, than are the other sources listed. It has the limitation of all private questionnaire surveys which cannot control the rate and the quality of the responses. It is believed that the bias in the purely quantitative responses which are used here is not great, if it exists at all, because there were pre-tests by interviews,

cross-checks comparing related questions in different parts of the questionnaire, checking with public sources, and correspondence with the firms
where any inconsistencies appeared.

6. A detailed empirical study for Australia was made recently by Donald T.
    Brash, entitled *American Investment in Australian Industry*. Questionnaire
    and interview techniques were used to examine the performance of 100
    companies in detail and, to a more limited extent, that of 108 other
    companies. The topics covered are similar to those listed in the foregoing
    paragraph but some are covered more broadly. The data refer mainly to the
    year 1962.

7. A detailed and very original study of the United Kingdom's experience was
    published a decade ago by John H. Dunning, entitled *American Investment
    in British Manufacturing Industry*. Interviews were conducted with the
    officers of 115 U.S. subsidiaries and 45 joint ventures, and mailed question-
    naires were used to secure data from 45 other firms. Both qualitative and
    quantitative information is supplied not only on topics noted above but
    particularly on the productivity of the subsidiaries and on their effects on
    those with whom they come in contact. The data refer mainly to experience
    in 1953-54. Early in 1969 Dunning published a study entitled *The Role of
    American Investment in the British Economy*, which summarizes and
    analyzes the results for the United Kingdom of his more recent empirical
    studies of this topic up to the years 1966-67.

BIBLIOGRAPHY

Books and Reports

Bonin, Bernard. *L'investissement étranger à long terme au Canada*. Montreal: Les Presses de l'Ecole des Hautes Etudes Commerciales de Montréal, 1967.

Brash, Donald T. *American Investment in Australian Industry*. Canberra: Australian National University Press, 1966.

Brecher, Irving, and Reisman, S. S. *Canada-United States Economic Relations*. Royal Commission on Canada's Economic Prospects, 1957.

Brewster, Kingman, Jr. *Law and United States Business in Canada*. Montreal and Washington: Canadian-American Committee, 1960.

Dunning, John H. *American Investment in British Manufacturing Industry*. London: George Allen and Unwin, 1958.

————. *The Role of American Investment in the British Economy*. London: Political and Economic Planning, 1969.

Eastman, H. C., and Stykolt, S. *The Tariff and Competition in Canada*. Toronto: Macmillan, 1967.

English, H. Edward. *Industrial Structure in Canada's International Competitive Position*. Montreal: Canadian Trade Committee, 1964.

Lea, Sperry. *Canada and the U.S. Capital Restraint Programs*. Montreal and Washington: Canadian-American Committee, forthcoming.

Lindeman, John, and Armstrong, Donald. *Policies and Practices of United States Subsidiaries in Canada*. Montreal and Washington: Canadian-American Committee, 1961.

Marshall, Herbert; Southard, Frank A., Jr.; and Taylor, Kenneth. *Canadian-American Industry*. New Haven: Yale University Press, 1936.

Porter, John. *The Vertical Mosaic: An Analysis of Social Class and Power in Canada*. Toronto: University of Toronto Press, 1965.

Safarian, A. E. *Foreign Ownership of Canadian Industry*. Toronto: McGraw-Hill Company of Canada Ltd., 1966.

Wilkinson, B. W. *Canada's International Trade: An Analysis of Recent Trends and Patterns*. Montreal: Canadian Trade Committee, 1968.

Articles

Arndt, H. W., and Sherk, D. R. "Export Franchises of Australian Companies with Overseas Affiliations," *The Economic Record*, August 1959, 239-42.

Gruber, William; Mehta, Dilheap; and Vernon, Raymond. "The R & D Factor in International Trade and International Investment of United States Industries," *The Journal of Political Economy*, February 1967.

Penrose, E. T. "Foreign Investment and the Growth of the Firm," *Economic Journal*, June 1956, 220-35.

Stykolt, Stefan, and Eastman, H. C. "A Model for the Study of Protected Oligopolies," *Economic Journal*, June 1960, 336-47.

Government Publications

Dominion Bureau of Statistics. *Corporations and Labour Unions Returns Act, Report for 1962* (1965), *Report for 1963* (1967), and *Report for 1964* (1969). Referred to as CALURA in footnotes and text. Ottawa: Queen's Printer.

_____ . *The Canadian Balance of International Payments, 1961 and 1962, and International Investment Position* (1964) and *1963, 1964, and 1965* (1967). Ottawa: Queen's Printer.

_____ . *Industrial Research and Development Expenditures in Canada.* Ottawa: Queen's Printer, 1965.

Dominion Bureau of Statistics and Department of Trade and Commerce. *Foreign-owned Subsidiaries in Canada.* Ottawa: Queen's Printer, 1967.

Organisation for Economic Co-operation and Development. *A Study of Resources Devoted to R and D in OECD Member Countries in 1963-64.* Paris, 1967.

Science Council of Canada, *First Annual Report*, 1966-67.

Task Force on the Structure of Canadian Industry. *Foreign Ownership and the Structure of Canadian Industry.* Prepared for the Privy Council Office. Ottawa: Queen's Printer, 1968.

U.S. Department of Commerce. *U.S. Business Investments in Foreign Countries.* A supplement to the *Survey of Current Business.* Washington: U.S. Government Printing Office, 1960.

_____ . *Survey of Current Business.* Various issues.

CANADIAN-AMERICAN COMMITTEE MEMBERS

Co-chairmen

ROBERT M. FOWLER
President, Canadian Pulp and Paper
Association, Montreal, Quebec

HAROLD W. SWEATT
Honorary Chairman of the Board,
Honeywell, Inc.
Minneapolis, Minnesota

Members

I. W. ABEL
President, United Steelworkers of
American, AFL-CIO, Pittsburgh,
Pennsylvania

T. N. BEAUPRE
Chairman of the Board and
President, Domtar Limited,
Montreal, Quebec

J. A. BEIRNE
President, Communications Workers
of America, AFL-CIO, Washington,
D.C.

T. J. BELL
President, Abitibi Paper Company
Ltd., Toronto, Ontario

WILLIAM J. BENNETT
President, Iron Ore Company of
Canada, Montreal, Quebec

HAROLD BOESCHENSTEIN
Chairman, Owens-Corning Fiberglas
Corporation, Toledo, Ohio

E. D. BROCKETT, JR.
Chairman of the Board,
Gulf Oil Corporation,
Pittsburgh, Pennsylvania

ARDEN BURBIDGE
Park River, North Dakota

EARL L. BUTZ
Vice President for Special Projects,
Purdue Research Foundation,
Lafayette, Indiana

FRANCOIS E. CLEYN
President, Cleyn & Tinker, Ltd.,
Huntingdon, Quebec

J. E. COUNTRYMAN
President, California Packing
Corporation, San Francisco,
California

THOMAS E. COVEL
Vice President, Aluminium Limited,
Inc., New York, New York

WILLIAM DODGE
Secretary-Treasurer, Canadian
Labour Congress, Ottawa, Ontario

A. D. DUNTON
President, Carleton University,
Ottawa, Ontario

H. E. EKBLOM
Senior Vice President, The Chase
Manhattan Bank, New York, New York

E. H. FALLON
Executive Vice President & General
Manager, Agway, Inc., Syracuse,
New York

MARCEL FARIBAULT
Montreal, Quebec

J. R. FLUOR
Chairman & Chief Executive Officer,
Fluor Corporation, Ltd.,
Los Angeles, California

HAROLD S. FOLEY
Vancouver, British Columbia

JOHN F. GALLAGHER
Vice President, International
Operations, Sears, Roebuck and Co.,
Chicago, Illinois

G.H. GALLAWAY
President,
Crown Zellerbach International,
Inc., San Francisco, California

ARTHUR R. GIBBONS
Executive Secretary, Canadian Railway
Labour Executives' Association, Ottawa,
Ontario

WILLIAM E. GRACE
President, Fruehauf Corporation,
Detroit, Michigan

W. N. HALL
Como, Quebec

JOHN A. HANNAH
Administrator, Agency for
International Development,
Washington, D.C.

F. PEAVEY HEFFELFINGER
Honorary Chairman of the Board
& Member of The Executive
Committee, Peavey Company,
Minneapolis, Minnesota

G. W. HUMPHREY
Chairman, The Hanna Mining
Company, Cleveland, Ohio

CURTIS M. HUTCHINS
Chairman of the Board, Dead River
Company, Bangor, Maine

R. A. IRWIN
President, Consolidated-Bathurst
Limited, Montreal, Quebec

GEORGE P. JENKINS
Chairman of the Finance Committee,
Metropolitan Life Insurance Company,
New York, New York

CRAWFORD T. JOHNSON
Assistant to the Chairman, Baker
Industries, New York, New York

VERNON E. JOHNSON
Calumet, Quebec

JOSEPH D. KEENAN
International Secretary, International
Brotherhood of Electrical Workers,
AFL-CIO, Washington, D.C.

DAVID KIRK
Executive Secretary, The Canadian
Federation of Agriculture, Ottawa,
Ontario

W. S. KIRKPATRICK
Chairman and Chief Executive
Officer, Cominco Ltd., Montreal,
Quebec

WILLIAM LADYMAN
International Vice President,
International Brotherhood of
Electrical Workers, AFL-CIO-CLC,
Toronto, Ontario

HERBERT H. LANK
Director, Du Pont of Canada, Limited,
Montreal, Quebec

FRANKLIN A. LINDSAY
President, Itek Corporation, Lexington,
Massachusetts

DONALD MacDONALD
President, Canadian Labour Congress,
Ottawa, Ontario

ROBERT P. MacFADDEN
Vice President, First National
City Bank, New York, New York

ROBERT M. MacINTOSH
Deputy Chief General Manager,
Bank of Nova Scotia, Toronto,
Ontario

M. W. MACKENZIE
Como, Quebec

W. A. MACKINTOSH
Kingston, Ontario

WILLIAM MAHONEY
National Director, United Steelworkers
of America, AFL-CIO-CLC, Toronto,
Ontario

*AUGUSTINE R. MARUSI
Chairman & President, Borden Inc.,
New York, New York

BROOKS McCORMICK
Executive Vice President,
International Harvester Company,
Chicago, Illinois

RALPH T. McELVENNY
President, American Natural Gas
Company, Detroit, Michigan

N. FLOYD McGOWIN
Chapman, Alabama

JOSEPH MORRIS
Executive Vice President, Canadian
Labour Congress, Ottawa, Ontario

KENNETH D. NADEN
Executive Vice President, National
Council of Farmer Cooperatives,
Washington, D.C.

THOMAS S. NICHOLS
Chairman of the Executive Committee,
Olin Mathieson Chemical Corporation,
New York, New York

JOSEPH E. NOLAN
Senior Vice President—
Administration,
Weyerhaeuser Company,
Tacoma, Washington

VICTOR deB. OLAND
Halifax, Nova Scotia

I. H. PECK
President, Canadian International
Paper Company, Montreal, Quebec

MARCEL PEPIN
National President, Confederation of
National Trade Unions, Montreal,
Quebec

CHARLES PERRAULT
Conseil du Patronat du Québec
Montreal, Quebec

R. E. POWELL
Honorary Chairman, Aluminum
Company of Canada, Limited,
Montreal, Quebec

HERBERT V. PROCHNOW
Honorary Director, The First
National Bank of Chicago,
Chicago, Illinois

GERARD RANCOURT
Executive Vice President, Canadian
Labour Congress, Ottawa, Ontario

*Not a member of the Canadian-American Committee when this publication was
circulated for signature.

JAY RODNEY REESE
President, Texas Instruments Supply
Company, Dallas, Texas

CHARLES RITZ
Honorary Chairman of the Board,
International Milling Company, Inc.,
Minneapolis, Minnesota

HOWARD I. ROSS
Touche, Ross, Bailey & Smart,
Montreal, Quebec

HENRY E. RUSSELL
President, Carling Brewing
Company, Cleveland, Ohio

THOMAS W. RUSSELL, JR.
First Vice President, Abex
Corporation, New York, New York

CLAUDE RYAN
Publisher-Editor, *Le Devoir*,
Montreal, Quebec

KARL E. SCOTT
President, Ford Motor Company of
Canada, Limited, Oakville, Ontario

L. D. SMITHERS
President, Dow Chemical of Canada,
Limited, Sarnia, Ontario

H. CHRISTIAN SONNE
New York, New York

CLAUDE O. STEPHENS
Chairman of the Board,
Texas Gulf Sulphur Company,
Incorporated, New York, New York

J. E. WALLACE STERLING
Chancellor, Stanford University,
Stanford, California

R. DOUGLAS STUART
Director, The Quaker Oats Company,
Chicago, Illinois

JAMES SUFFRIDGE
International President Emeritus,
Retail Clerks International
Association,
AFL-CIO, Washington, D.C.

A. W. TARKINGTON
President, Continental Oil Company,
New York, New York

W. P. TAVOULAREAS
Executive Vice President, Mobil
Oil Corporation, New York, New York

W. I. M. TURNER, JR.
President, Power Corporation of
Canada, Limited, Montreal, Quebec

W. O. TWAITS
President, Imperial Oil Limited
Toronto, Ontario

J. R. WHITE
Vice President and Director, Standard
Oil Company (New Jersey), New York,
New York

HENRY S. WINGATE
Chairman, The International Nickel
Company of Canada, Limited, New
York, New York

FRANCIS G. WINSPEAR
Chartered Accountant and Company
Director, Edmonton, Alberta

DAVID J. WINTON
The Winton Company, Minneapolis,
Minnesota

ARNOLD S. ZANDER
Green Bay, Wisconsin

PUBLICATIONS OF THE CANADIAN-AMERICAN COMMITTEE*

Other Publications on the Investment Relationship

Law and United States Business in Canada, by Kingman Brewster, Jr. This report examines the alleged extraterritorial application of U.S. law to U.S. firms doing business in Canada. It then attempts to describe the U.S. policy purposes and the bases of Canadian resentment in two of the more significant fields of legal conflict: anti-trust and cold-war trade controls. 1960, 40 pages, $1.00.

Policies and Practices of U.S. Subsidiaries in Canada, by John Lindeman and Donald Armstrong. This report surveys six aspects of business motivated subsidiary behaviour that have provoked the most critical comment among Canadians: public sale of equity shares; Canadianization of personnel; publication of financial data; marketing and purchasing policies; research policies; and philanthropic activities. 1961, 94 pages, $2.00.

Recent Canadian and U.S. Government Actions Affecting U.S. Investment in Canada, Staff Study. A factual account of the Canadian budget proposal of 1963 and the subsequent U.S. Interest Equalization Tax proposal and their separate implications for various forms of U.S. investment in Canada. The publication includes the Committee's previously issued policy statement, "Preserving the Canada-U.S. Common Market for Capital." 1964, 27 pages, $1.00.

Capital Flows Between Canada and the United States, by Irving Brecher. A comprehensive description of the full range of capital movements in terms of the statistics of both countries. The report explores the reasons for the shifting pattern of flows and such issues as Canadian exchange rate policy and the U.S. program of 1965 to curtail private investment outflow. 1965, 141 pages, $2.00.

Commercial Relations

The Growth and Changing Composition of Trade Between Canada and the United States, by Grant L. Reuber. 1960 ($2.00)

Barriers to Trade Between Canada and the United States, by Francis Masson and J. B. Whitely. 1960 ($2.00)

Changes in Trade Restrictions Between Canada and the United States, by Constant Southworth and W. W. Buchanan. 1960 ($2.00)

The U.S. Trade Expansion Act of 1962: How Will It Affect Canadian-American Trade? by Howard S. Piquet. 1963 ($2.00)

Non-Merchandise Transactions Between Canada and the United States, by John W. Popkin. 1963 ($1.50)

Invisible Trade Barriers Between Canada and the United States, by Francis Masson and H. Edward English. 1963 ($1.50)

A Canada-U.S. Free Trade Arrangement: Survey of Possible Characteristics, by Sperry Lea. 1963 ($2.00)

A Possible Plan for a Canada-U.S. Free Trade Area, a Staff Report. 1965 ($1.50)

A New Trade Strategy for Canada and the United States, a Statement by the Committee. 1966 ($1.00)

Constructive Alternatives to Proposals for U.S. Import Quotas, a Statement by the Committee. 1968 ($1.00)

U.S.-Canadian Free Trade: The Potential Impact on the Canadian Economy, by Paul Wonnacott and Ronald J. Wonnacott. 1968 ($1.50)

Basic Commodities

Wheat Surpluses and Their Impact on Canada-United States Relations, by W. E. Hamilton and W. M. Drummond. 1959 ($1.00)

Oil and Canada-United States Relations, by John Davis. 1959 ($1.00)

Natural Gas and Canada-United States Relations, by John Davis. 1959 ($1.00)

Towards a Solution of Our Wheat Surplus Problems, a Statement by the Committee. 1959 (30c)

Wanted: A Working Environment More Conducive to Canadian-American Trade in Natural Gas, a Statement by the Committee. 1959 (25c)

Wheat Surpluses and the U.S. Barter Program, a Statement by the Committee. 1960 (35c)

The Future of Industrial Raw Materials in North America, by Wilbert G. Fritz. 1960 ($2.00)

The U.S. Softwood Lumber Situation in a Canadian-American Perspective, by Sperry Lea. 1962 ($1.00)

External Relations

The Growth of Soviet Economic Power and Its Consequences for Canada and the United States, by Franklin A. Lindsay. 1959 ($1.00)

Canada's Trade with Cuba and Canadian-American Relations, a Statement by the Committee (mimeographed). 1961 (50c)

Canada and the Organization of American States, by John D. Harbron. 1963 ($1.00)

Other

Cooperative Development of the Columbia River Basin, a Statement by the Committee. 1960 (25c)

The Perspective of Canadian-American Relations, a Statement by the Committee. 1962 (75c)

The Role of International Unionism in Canada, by John H. G. Crispo. 1967
   ($1.50)

*These publications may be ordered from the Committee's offices at 1606 New Hampshire Avenue, N.W., Washington, D.C. 20009, and at 757 Sun Life Building, Montreal 110, Quebec. Quantity discounts are given. A descriptive flyer of these publications is also available.

NATIONAL PLANNING ASSOCIATION

The National Planning Association was founded in 1934 as an independent, private, non-profit, and non-political organization. It engages in studies and develops recommendations on major policy issues confronting the United States, both in domestic affairs and in international relations. Its research provides information and methodologies valuable to public and private decision-makers.

NPA is governed by a Board of Trustees representing all private sectors of the American economy — business, labor, farm, and the professions. The Steering Committee of the Board, the four Standing Committees (the Agriculture, Business, and Labor Committees on National Policy, and the Committee on International Policy), and Special Policy Committees (including the Canadian-American Committee) originate and approve NPA policy statements and reports. Major research projects undertaken for government and international agencies, and through foundation grants, are carried out with the guidance of research advisory committees providing the best knowledge available. The full-time staff of the Association as of June 15, 1969, totaled 96 professional and administrative personnel.

The Association has a public membership of some 3,000 individuals, corporations, organizations, and groups. NPA activities are financed by contributions from individuals, business firms, trade unions, and farm organizations; by grants for particular research projects from private foundations; and by research contracts with Federal, state, and local government agencies and international organizations.

PRIVATE PLANNING ASSOCIATION OF CANADA

The Private Planning Association of Canada is a private, non-political, non-profit organization created in 1958 for the purpose of undertaking independent and objective studies of Canadian problems and policies, mainly in the fields of economic affairs and of Canada's international relationships with other countries.

The Association is sponsored by a large number of private donors, including business firms, labour unions, and agricultural federations, who make annual financial contributions in support of its work. Specific study projects and programs have, from time to time, also received assistance from foundations and from federal and provincial government agencies.

A large part of the work of the Association is carried on under the auspices of Committees, composed of agricultural, business, educational, labour, and professional leaders who meet to consider important national issues and to sponsor and review studies that contribute to better public understanding of such issues. At present there are two of these Committees. One is the Canadian Economic Policy Committee, which was formed in 1969 by expansion of the terms of reference of the former Canadian Trade Committee. The other is the Canadian-American Committee, sponsored jointly by the National Planning Association in Washington. The publications of both Committees are available from the Association's office, 757 Sun Life Building, Montreal 110, Quebec (Tel. 514-861-6319).